Elderburbia

Elderburbia

Aging with a Sense of Place in America

PHILIP B. STAFFORD

Foreword by Scott Russell Sanders

PRAEGER

An Imprint of ABC-CLIO, LLC

A B C  C L I O

Santa Barbara, California • Denver, Colorado • Oxford, England

Library of Congress Cataloging-in-Publication Data

Stafford, Philip B.
   Elderburbia : aging with a sense of place in America / Philip B. Stafford ;
   foreword by Scott Russell Sanders.
     p. cm.
   Includes bibliographical references and index.
   ISBN 978–0–313–36436–5 (hbk. : alk. paper) — ISBN 978–0–313–36437–2 (ebook)
1. Aging—United States. 2. Older people—Housing—United States. 3. Older people—Services for
—United States. 4. Community development—United States. 5. Suburbs—United States.
6. Retirement communities—United States. I. Title.
HQ1064.U5S6822   2009
305.260973—dc22   2009026679

13 12 11 10 09   1 2 3 4 5

This book is also available on the World Wide Web as an eBook.
Visit www.abc-clio.com for details.

ABC-CLIO, LLC
130 Cremona Drive, P.O. Box 1911
Santa Barbara, California 93116-1911

To Linda, in whose love I dwell

Contents

Foreword

Throughout our history, Americans have tended to be infatuated with movement and fearful of settlement. Our mythology celebrates pilgrims, explorers, cowboys, prospectors, and pioneers, while it warns us against being trapped on a farm, in a hollow, in a puritanical village, or in a stifling city. We associate moving on with adventure and freedom, while we associate staying put with confinement and backwardness. Such a bias toward mobility makes sense for a young nation composed of immigrants and the descendants of immigrants, with most of a continent to populate and with vast natural wealth to exploit.

But America has long since become densely populated, and indeed by some measures it is overpopulated, while the continent's natural wealth has been claimed or exhausted. Nearly four centuries after the establishment of permanent European colonies on the Atlantic seaboard, more than two centuries after the founding of the United States, we are no longer a young nation, and we need a culture that reflects our increasing maturity, one that values settlement at least as highly as it values movement. At long last, we should recognize that the alternative to mobility need not be stagnation, but may be a deep and fulfilling engagement with place.

Philip Stafford has documented just how vital such an engagement with place is, especially for older people. He shows that "place" may be understood at various scales, from a favorite easy chair to a house, a city, or a countryside. Objects, buildings, streets, and landscapes take on meaning for us when they are saturated with stories, both the stories we have lived and those we have learned. The longer we dwell in a place, the deeper our memories become, and the richer our sense of belonging. We come to recognize the cycle of the seasons, the look of thunderclouds and the shiver of hard rain, the sound of church bells or train whistles, the odors from a tire shop or a bakery, the taste of tap water or persimmon pudding. We know the neighbors and the neighborhood. This knowledge grounds us, the way roots nourish and steady a tree. Indoors, the well-thumbed books on our shelves, the mementoes from travels, the comfortable old jacket hanging on a hook by the back door, the potted fern our son or daughter once gave us for a birthday, the crayoned drawings from grandchildren, all of these remind us of who we are, what we have accomplished, whom we love, and who loves us in turn.

As we age, a sense of belonging to place, of being at home, enables us to remain more fully ourselves, even while certain of our powers may diminish. In the words of one older woman quoted by Stafford, "When you're home, you're whole. You're a whole person." Drawing on the latest research on aging, and on his own landmark studies, Stafford enlarges our understanding of what "home" can mean for the elderly. He describes a variety of living arrangements and social amenities that allow elders to enjoy the greatest sense of autonomy, creativity, and well-being in their late years. All of us are destined to become elders, if we live long enough, so all of us have reason to welcome this discerning and compassionate book.

Scott Russell Sanders
Department of English
Indiana University, Bloomington, Indiana

Acknowledgments

My fascination with the subject of aging in the community goes back decades. To acknowledge with appreciation the many people who have shared their lives and their collegiality with me would take pages and pages. I would start, however, with my own close Indiana University colleagues at the Center on Aging and Community, Indiana Institute on Disability and Community, Jane Harlan-Simmons, Peg Holtz, Jim McCorkle, Maribeth Mooney, Jennie Todd, and Lora Wagers. They have been an ongoing source of intellectual stimulation and very kind to understand the recent closed-door policy that has enabled me to wrap things up. Their creative work in helping to improve the quality of life for adults aging with disabilities in Indiana has been significant, and should be a model for other states to follow. Institute Director David Mank provides an incredibly supportive collegial environment to enable all of us to excel.

It seems that within each organization I have worked over the past 30 years, I have been extremely fortunate to be a member of a team that possessed energy, creativity, endurance, and great humor. At Evergreen Institute this included Janet Barrows, Jane Clay, Karen Danielson, Bridget Edwards, Nicole Kousaleos, Erica Peterson-Veatch, Julianne Short, and an incredible board of advisors. At Bloomington Hospital this included Jody Curley, Laura Diven-Brown, and Julie Hill. At South Central Community Mental Health Center this included Loretta Armer, Mona Harmon-Bowman, Gordon Gibson, Walt Keller, Dixie Kline-Richardson, Jane Norris, and Gal Shifron. I know I overlook others who have, with these friends, played an instrumental role in helping me think through, and work through, multiple issues around health, mental health, and the role of community institutions in the lives of older persons.

Intellectual mentors and colleagues to whom I owe deep gratitude include Judith Hansen, Tom Sebeok (both gone now), Allen Grimshaw, Henry Glassie, Anya Royce, Inta Carpenter, Scott Russell Sanders, Jay Sokolovsky, Maria Vesperi, Jaber Gubrium, Joel Savishinsky, Graham Rowles, Neil Henderson, and other members of the Association for Anthropology and Gerontology too numerous to mention. All of these individuals have inspired me over the years as I have tried to formulate and articulate an approach to aging that seeks to understand the subjective lifeworld of individual elders, while drawing lessons about the importance of preserving place and sustaining community memory.

The AdvantAge Initiative, nationally, and its Indiana iteration, has provided me the opportunity to learn from a host of impressive professionals in the aging network, Duane Etienne, Anne Jacoby, David Hanson, John Beilensen, Stephanie Pinder, Jan Hively, Dace Kramer, the Indiana advisory group, and my friends at the Center for Aging and Community, University of Indianapolis.

I and my associates could not have pursued what is currently the most exciting chapter in my life—working on the transformation of communities—without funding support from the Retirement Research Foundation (for the Evergreen Project); the Daniels Fund of Denver, Colorado; Lilly Endowment, Inc.; the U.S. Administration on Aging; Indiana Family and Social Services Administration; Indiana Agencies on Aging; and Indiana University. This work connects me with a group of friends and colleagues who are going to change the world—Mia Oberlink, Kathryn Lawler, Laura Bly, and Fredda Vladeck. Stay tuned for more.

I am truly blessed to live in a community that is itself a good place to grow up and grow old. It holds people in place, including my dear ones —wife, Linda, to whom the book is dedicated, daughters Libby and Abby, grandchildren Jayden and Mya. And it has provided a home for our family as it ages, giving me the good fortune to remain close to my late mother Joanna R. Stafford and mother-in-law Louise (Mrs. Ken) Norris, not to mention sister, brother, nieces, and nephew. Who would have thought we would all end up in the same community!

Appreciation is extended to SAR Press, Praeger Publishers, and Indiana University Press for permission to reprint, with revisions, portions of chapters published elsewhere. Portions of Chapter 1 were published as "Homebodies: Voices of Place in a North American Community," in *Gray Areas: Ethnographic Encounters with Nursing Home Culture*, ed. P. Stafford (Santa Fe, NM: SAR Press, 2003). Portions of Chapter 2 were published as "Living Large while Living Small: The Spatial Life of Aging Boomers," in *Boomer Bust? Economic and Political Issues of the Graying Society*, Volume Two, ed. R. B. Hudson (Westport, CT: Praeger, 2008). An excerpt from "Town Squares," entry for *The American Midwest: An Interpretive Encyclopedia*, ed. R. Sisson, C. Zacher, and A. Cayton (Bloomington, IN: Indiana University Press, 2006), is included in Chapter 6. Portions of Chapter 5 and Chapter 9 were derived from papers presented at meetings of the American Anthropological Association.

Finally I must express my deepest gratitude for the friendship and inspiration of those elders in the Bloomington area who, from first to last, have contributed so much to my professional and personal growth, with special appreciation to Roy and Margaret Ballinger, Myron and Nee Howard, Lloyd Johnson, Esther Sturgeon, Milton Figen, and Elizabeth Bridgwaters, all of whom have passed on to the next great adventure.

Introduction: The Demographic Imperative

For decades, America's promise has been the suburb—tidy houses, green lawns, and backyard barbeques, conveniently distant from noxious industries and urban congestion. A home in the country—sort of.

This image, along with a massive program of public support, lured millions who could afford it away from traditional urban spaces. The trend started in the 1950s as postwar families soaked up VA and FHA home loans in tract subdivisions, while envisioning easy commutes in stylish new cars along gleaming "Eisenhower" highways.

This trend is familiar to us all. What is less well-recognized, perhaps, is that this trend has continued to this day. Not only did families with young children flock to the suburbs, but young adults, now called Baby Boomers, have maintained this pattern to the present. Not only have those 1950s parents grown old in their suburbs, but Baby Boomers have joined them there. Now, more older people live in suburbs than in cities and towns combined! This is Elderburbia. As a suburban phenomenon, then, we must ask, "is the suburb a good place to grow old?"

Clean air and green grass notwithstanding, I am afraid we cannot answer that question in the affirmative.

The suburb isolates elders who do not drive from essential community services and amenities.

For elders who do drive, the suburban development pattern creates a reliance on major arterials for connections to commerce and work, arterials that become ever-more congested and dangerous for drivers with lower vision and slower reaction times.

In suburbs where culs-de-sac have replaced traditional street grids, it becomes cost-prohibitive to provide public transit services, where larger vehicles cannot turn around nor make efficient runs.

In suburbs that have grown old due to the loss of children (naturally occurring retirement communities), old people are left with each other alone, cut off from the supportive labor of young persons and life-affirming relationships with children.

In suburbs where every yard is fenced, houses without porches are set back from the sidewalk, and garage doors open and close at the flick of a button, elders (and others) are totally relieved of the need for or opportunity of interacting face-to-face with neighbors.

In suburbs where every house is of similar vintage and style and where every trace of geological and historical past has been erased, it would not occur to visit an elderly neighbor to tap the memory of the place. There is no memory of the place.

In suburbs where every lot is large by design and covenants require upkeep, the frail elder risks being ostracized for not keeping up her place and, personally, takes it to heart when she looks out her window at weedy flower beds that were once a source of pride.

In Peter Pan suburbs where houses were designed as if no one would grow old, the frail elder struggles with a bathroom that does not admit her walker or a bathtub that makes it impossible to bathe her husband with dementia.

In suburbs where covenants and municipal laws preclude changes to the footprint and the composition of the house, older people are prevented from adding on a caregiver unit, taking in a boarder, or perhaps even having an extra car parked on the street for an aide.

In the recent past, increasing suburban property values have made it more and more difficult for elders on fixed incomes to keep up with property taxes, let alone the increasing costs associated with what may be aging housing stock.

In short, if the suburb is to ever complete its promise, it will require some massive retrofitting as America ages.

But this book is only in part about Elderburbia. There are others who have written with more expertise than I on the kind of retrofitting that will be needed to make the suburbs work for people as they age (Dunham-Jones and Williamson 2009; Abbott et al. 2009).

This book is about achieving a more fundamental goal. It is not about the spaces where older people live, so much as about the places they call home. It suggests that home is not just a house, an apartment, a flat, but an accomplishment. It is about homemaking ... not in the traditional sense of washing, ironing, scrubbing, but in its more basic sense as dwelling, as belonging, as, in Michael Jackson's words, "being at home in the world" (1995).

For this book, I have drawn on my three decades of research about and practice with older people, and young ones too. And I should probably extend that range to nearly 60 years, for, as long as I can remember, I have been fascinated by the stories told by older people in my neighborhood(s). One of my earliest memories is of visiting across the street with an ancient Mrs. Culbertson, who was a direct descendant of Daniel Boone.

Because this topic is of such high personal importance, I have inserted myself into the argument, offering a first person view of aging in the concluding chapter. Indeed, I would highly recommend the study of aging to any young person entering a new career *because* the personal rewards are so great, not to mention that the professional opportunities are growing every year. They are growing because of the demographic imperative— the graying of America and the world. Some have referred to this phenomenon as a "silver tsunami." Peter Peterson, evoking potential generational conflict, has referred to the upcoming "gray dawn" in the bleakest terms. He says "we face a threat more grave and certain than those posed by chemical weapons, nuclear proliferation, or ethnic strife: the 'age wave'" (1999). Others, fortunately, have begun exploring the possibility that the coming age wave may not be the end of the world as we know it but, rather, a wonderful opportunity.

> Our enormous and rapidly growing older population is a vast, untapped social resource. If we can engage these individuals in ways that fill urgent gaps in our society, the result will be a windfall for American civic life in the twenty-first century. (Freedman 1999)

Whether the interpretation is catastrophic, as with Peterson, or optimistic, as with Marc Freedman, the imperative to prepare is obvious. The numbers hardly bear repeating. Suffice it to say that there are currently more seniors in the United States than people in the entire country of Canada, and that this number will increase 147 percent by 2050, when 21 percent of the U.S. population will be 65 or older (U.S. Census

2008). The entire country will look like Florida . . . sort of (aging is not uniform across the landscape).

If Florida is in our future, just how shall we prepare? That is the challenge taken up in this book.

Many current popular works on the subject see the challenge as an individual one, as it certainly is. We have lotions and potions, nips and tucks, diets and pills to keep us young. We have antiaging medicine and magical villages where no one grows old. More power to them, though I have to say, it is a losing battle. We do grow old. We die. The best we can hope for, and perhaps influence, is to "square the curve"—be as vital and healthy as we can till we drop out of this life.

In the concluding chapter I offer a personal philosophy that addresses these sometimes unwelcome vicissitudes of old age. But my philosophy about aging is that it is not about time and the body, but about place, and relationships. Aging, illness, and disability are not in the body but in the *relationship* between the body and its environment. Aging is, so to speak, an out-of-body experience. Moreover, we do not merely exist in a Skinnerian environment where brute forces are at work—a stimulus/response scenario. We live in an environment of meaning, wrapped within what Clifford Geertz called "webs of significance" (1973). Nor do we face aging alone. Just as we make meaning together, we face aging within communities and, so, this is the challenge taken up in this book: how can our communities prepare for the aging of our society?

As a community project, and not simply an individual one, we need to find ways to work together to create good places to grow old. The first step is to listen deeply to better understand the aging experience from the inside, to come to grips with the daily lifeworld of elders. Chapter 1, "Being and Dwelling in Old Age," draws upon ethnographic research to interpret the deep and profound meanings of home in the lives of mostly midwestern elders. Not presuming to understand aging in highly urbanized cities nor in totally rural environments, I offer a picture of what it is like to grow old in a fairly common small city, in established prewar neighborhoods with modest homes and traditional grid streets and alleys —what many New Urbanists would see as ideal urban form. While the formerly ubiquitous corner groceries have faded away, these neighborhoods still work pretty well as places to grow old. Attachment to place is strong. Neighborly relationships are fairly intact or, at least, still exist in recent memory.

While these neighborhoods occupy a favored position in my hierarchy of places, I try to remain open-minded about the kinds of location choices that older adults make in retirement. Chapter 2, "Locating Old Age," surveys the array of choices made by those who select to relocate in old age. These are the images bombarding us in the popular media—Sun City, the Villages, Retire to Reno! While noting that most people *do not* relocate in retirement, but remain in the suburbs, the chapter suggests that the old Sun City, gated-community model of old age may be on the way out.

Chapters 3 and 4 offer some approaches that begin to demonstrate how communities might set about the work of preparing themselves for the demographic changes in store. The AdvantAge Initiative (AI) is one approach that provides a solid framework for systematic, evidence-based community planning. Organized around a scientific survey process now completed in multiple cities, regions, and nationally, the AI model has the potential to provide the comprehensive information needed to assist municipalities in rational planning toward improved environments for aging. Chapter 3 concludes with some observations about how change occurs in communities and what leadership qualities are essential to make it happen.

Chapter 4 illustrates the limits of data and the necessity to develop community participation processes that complement the numbers and provide the interpretations that make the numbers come alive in stories. I argue that participation is a necessary tool of democracy and offer multiple examples that can be tried in other settings.

Much of the literature in the current "elder-friendly," "age-friendly" movement has focused on the concrete steps that can be taken to create communities that work across the lifespan. We talk about good sidewalks, diverse housing options, safe streets, quality health care, senior facilities. Less often do we discuss the intangibles—the less visible elements that play a critical role in placemaking. Chapters 5 and 6 try to redress the balance, arguing that memory, on the one hand, and sociability, on the other, are hallmarks of a good place to grow old, or grow up for that matter. Many communities these days exhibit their own brand of dementia, writ large. Their residents do not possess nor sustain a memory of the place. As such, many places exist out of time, which, I imagine, is just another manifestation of our collective denial of aging. In Chapter 5, I offer some examples of methods that communities can employ to sustain community memory and note that such projects often have, as a consequence, the valorization of the role that elders can and should play in a good community.

Chapter 6 illuminates what actually transpires in those spots that have come to be known as "third places"—those nonwork, nonhome spaces where people engage in good company. These sometimes spontaneous, sometimes traditional spaces far outnumber the programmed spaces in which we typically picture senior citizens. They are "beyond bingo" spaces out of reach of the recreation specialists. Being "naturally occurring," emergent places, they have not been much discussed within the discipline of gerontology. Ironically, they are likely known by us all and intuitively recognized when we see them or have the good fortune to join them. Chapter 6 takes the reader to the daily coffee club of a small midwestern town, to join the local ROMEOS—retired old men eating out —and learn what makes it a satisfying place to be.

Chapter 7 continues to explore emergent forms of aging, where old people themselves are taking hold of their own destiny and eschewing the grasp of the programmers and the marketers. It provides a glimpse into new forms of association that small groups of elders are forming to meet their changing needs in the face of aging. Based on brief trips to Dakota County, Minnesota, and Boulder, Colorado, the chapter looks at innovative projects in which elders are moving collectively to design new approaches to supportive services and housing.

Chapter 8 integrates information about the lifeworld of elders, community planning, and the intangibles of good places to sketch a picture of the new Elderburbia, where communities are radically transformed from isolating spaces to authentic places in which elders thrive as essential players in communities for life. In the concluding chapter I try to piece together some lessons for myself (and significant others) as I age and, as authors are privileged to do, some prescriptions for the future.

Throughout, I intersperse a few vignettes, all true, that seemed too important, but perhaps too lengthy, to incorporate into the text. I have been so very privileged to know people willing to share their experiences and their lives with me as they moved through time. It is my hope that this book blends the personal and the professional in such a way as to make a contribution to the understanding of a phenomenon that, by its very nature, none of us escapes, if we are fortunate enough.

CHAPTER 1

Being and Dwelling in Old Age

There was a time when I bought into the notion that old age was a period of stability, even an ending of sorts. Old people themselves sometimes mark late life as a place to stop and rest. Picture an elderly couple swaying on their porch swing and waving as you fly by in your car, highlighting your motion in the face of their stasis. Too bad, you think. There they sit waiting for someone to come brighten up their staid lives, stuck in place.

So I might have thought before coming into regular contact with Margaret and Roy Ballinger, my wife's grandparents. Yes, they spent many hours sitting on the porch swing on Central Avenue in Worthington, Indiana. Only when I spent time with them myself did I come to understand how active their lives were, that the porch swing itself was the base from which they sustained an active social life and remained connected in the community. Regular weekend visits with Margaret and Roy provided a wonderful dose of reality in my life as a frazzled graduate student.

Margaret and Roy were well positioned. The street leading into town saw regular traffic, slowing a bit as it approached the bend near the grain elevator and the adjoining railroad crossing. Indeed, the traffic slowed enough to get a clear view of the vehicle's occupants and, often, a few seconds to establish the eye contact necessary for a knowing exchange of glances and even words through an open window.

Occasionally, between carefully planned thrusts with his fly swatter, Roy would verbally sketch a portrait of the person, couple, or family we observed driving by. We became privy to work habits, genealogies, marriage and divorce histories, and amusing episodes in the lives of

Worthingtonians. I recall the old fellow who meandered by on a pony cart heading downtown one Saturday afternoon. "He's straight for the tavern," Roy explained. "He's the town drunk and had his driver's license removed. It didn't stop him." I also remember the little man who would carry a broom and sweep the sidewalk in front of him as he headed for town. Margaret explained his routine to us. He swept all the way to the park, where he would stop, urinate against a tree, and sweep back home again. Why he swept his way downtown was not an issue, nor was his unusual behavior a cause for alarm. That was just what he did. A character, for sure, but a lovable one accepted by all.

On many occasions, people would stop and sit a spell. Chairs would be pulled into the yard under the cool shade of a large maple. If sweet corn needed shucking or beans needed snapping, Grandma Ballinger would carry bowls of it out to the collection of people in the yard. Simple and satisfying conversation was the rule. Politics was not off limits, though when Uncle Charles stopped by we all made an effort to avoid getting him going on that subject. Not infrequently, small children would stop on the way home from school or, in the summertime, from the river. Grandma and Grandpa dispensed much sage advice to the little ones about how to fend off bullies and older brothers and sisters.

In short, life on the porch swing was lively and full, not lonely and dull. How wrong it would be to fly by in a fast car and denigrate the idea of aging in place. Life, "from the inside," is always more complex than we assume.

Research we have conducted in Bloomington, Indiana (Stafford 2001), suggests that the concept of home—the meaning of home for older people—is deep and multifaceted. From 1995 to 1997 our small team of ethnographers spent hundreds of hours conducting in-depth interviews in the home and accompanying elders on their ordinary quotidian routines. We collected oral histories. We explored the physical environments of the houses, the yards, the neighborhoods, and the larger community of Bloomington in tandem with our informants. We conducted focus groups, writing groups, and design workshops (charrettes) with dozens of elders, joining in a dialogue to discuss problems, values, community assets, and a vision for a good place to grow old. Over the course of two years, nearly 1,000 Bloomington elders joined the participatory research project. (The nature and value of the research methodology is further discussed in Chapter 8.) The research contributed to a deeper understanding of the meaning of home and domestic life for Bloomington elders. Some fundamental points are asserted herewith.

HOME IS REPLETE WITH MEANING AND MEMORY

Sediments of meaning and memory are laid down over time when we dwell in a place. And in Bloomington, we are talking about a long period of time. Among participants in our household survey project of 200 randomly selected elders in Bloomington, the average tenure in the home was 30 years, with a range of 11 months to 75 years! One can hardly imagine the rich archaeology of memory associated with such a longtime occupation in place. As one older widower explained to a group of youths working with our research team, "My home? It's my wife, my kitchen with big bay window, history with children at home, the smell of cut grass."

For him, ordinary events and actions are inscribed into the physical environment of the house. As he moves through the house he revisits the experiences, the thoughts, the feelings associated with family life. The walls, the objects, the yard, the furnishings have been infused with meaning, though he may be the sole remaining interpreter of these idiosyncracies. For this gentleman, revisiting the life of the place brings joy and also pain, yet he would have it no other way.

The house as place becomes a mirror for the self, a theme explored deeply by Clare Cooper Marcus in a book of the same title (1995). Through an extensive series of interviews over 20 years, the author examines multiple themes of homemaking across the lifespan: the remembrance of special childhood places, inhabited and created and, sometimes, endured; leaving home and the associated developmental tasks of entering adulthood; the negotiation of territory among those who live together; the loss of home through divorce, death of another, institutionalization. Throughout, Marcus relies on a Jungian premise, suggesting that the personalization of space is part of a universal psychological process, much of it unconscious, in which our selves strive toward wholeness and integration. Where many have explored this process in terms of how we invest emotionally in others, Marcus's contribution is found in demonstrating how we invest emotionally in objects and places.

For the adult child attempting to assist an older parent with getting rid of "all that stuff," the story is a familiar one. Throwing away an object can be the equivalent of throwing away a memory, or even throwing away a life. Objects themselves may exhibit no trace of intrinsic value, while being of incalculable worth to the owner. Differential perspectives on the "worth" of these objects can surface tension and emotion, marking an important developmental challenge within the family.

Ekerdt and Sargent use the term "disbandment" to refer to the process of reducing the volume of possessions in the course of a residential move (2006, 193). Acknowledging previous research on the manner in which "things" take on symbolic import (e.g., Csikszentmihalyi and Rochberg-Halton 1981), or function to sustain or create a legacy or memorialization (Marcoux 2001), the authors focus attention on the actual family dynamics of the management and dispossession of objects. Though rarely an easy, nonemotional task, whether it happens before or after the death of an elder parent, the interaction itself contributes to the very core process through which a family takes on a view of itself:

> family willingness to help does affirm mutual ties and establish who helps whom, who is central, and who is marginal. Deeper involvement becomes an occasion to later recall the way "we" cooperated, or how "we" got it done, or how "we" squabbled in our usual way. The elder's offer of cherished possessions might signal who is regarded as "in" a family and who is not. The reception of cherished possessions further constitutes family by reminding the participants that the collective has boundaries outside of which some belongings must not fall. Their retention within the family also signals that it endures and remembers. [The process] ... is a resource for telling "who we are." (Ekerdt and Sargent 2006, 204)

Many elders with whom I have talked have reached a certain level of acceptance regarding the loss of things. It is said that while it is important to be among "your things," it is unrealistic to think that one can bring everything along. *How* one separates from things, though, can make a difference. Some concern about the disposition of one's things, for example, is reflected in the violent phrase so commonly used to describe the event of "breaking up the home." This loss is mitigated significantly if the owner is able to exert some control over where things go. Anna Simpson described to me the systematic method by which she distributed family heirlooms upon her entry into the residential wing of a long-term care facility. She speaks highly of those younger heirs who can be trusted to "keep things in the family." The importance of this control is reflected in Anna's willingness to continue to pay rent on her apartment for three months after she moved—enough time to carefully distribute the furnishings. For some residents the luxury of time in these circumstances is limited, as long-distance family members may sweep into town for a few days to get this done all at once and get back to their own lives. The process must feel more violent when it happens that way.

The prospect of knowing the persons who inherit one's things must ameliorate the loss, a point noted by Marcus as well (1995, 246). Not knowing who is getting your things suggests an exacerbation of grief. Korosec-Serfaty, though she is speaking of the experience of being burglarized, summarizes some of the implications of this loss:

> The word *rape* (used by interviewees who had been burglarized) moreover emphasizes the articulations of the home experience and the body-as-self. The articulation appears, on the one hand, at the level of *sight* and, on the other hand, at the level of *touch*. Says a 40-year old man:
>
>> They've violated our privacy, these people who broke in here. We tell ourselves, well they *saw* things which belong to us, which are, well they're our own little secrets, they're not anybody's business; we don't tell them to anyone. That's it, it's this aspect of the thing, rather than what they stole.
>
> This foreign gaze, imposed, loaded with deceit ("we've certainly been watched"), ransacks what is nobody's business and which is generally closed: the boxes, chests, drawers, closets, and the dressing table, where you always keep a few things (60 year-old woman). (1985, 78)

Insofar as we can become attached to a dwelling, the feel of the house becomes as much a part of us as its surface appearances. Indeed, we can walk through a familiar place with our eyes closed not because we hold consciously to a cognitive representation of it, but because our *bodies* know the place. It becomes a part of our *habitus*. Bachelard, for example, describes this process through which so-called mundane household routines enter into our being and take on a reality not appreciated by those who would separate work from play, work from life. Quoting Henri Bosco, the quiet and persistent work of the old servant Sidoine is described:

> The soft wax entered into the polished substance under the pressure of hands and the effective warmth of a woolen cloth. Slowly the tray took on a dull luster. It was as though the

radiance induced by magnetic rubbing emanated from the hundred-year-old sapwood, from the very heart of the dead tree, and spread gradually, in the form of light, over the tray. The old fingers possessed of every virtue, the broad palm, drew from the solid block with its inanimate fibers, the latent powers of life itself. This was creation of an object, a real act of faith taking place before my enchanted eyes. (Bachelard 1994, 68)

As Bachelard describes the intimate daily process of building a house "from the inside," so Wendell Berry, in his novel *The Memory of Old Jack*, beautifully describes the process by which the old Kentucky farmer Jack Beechum melds with the landscape around him.

He had known no other place. From babyhood he had moved in the openings and foldings of the old farm as familiarly as he moved inside his clothes. Before he bought it he had farmed it for five years as the tenant of the other heirs. But after the full responsibility of it fell to him, he saw it with a new clarity. He had simply relied on it before. Now when he walked in his fields and pastures and woodlands he was tramping into his mind the shape of the land, his thought becoming indistinguishable from it, so that when he came to die, his intelligence would subside into it like his own spirit. (Berry 1974, 30)

These are Jack's fields, yes, but they are not his *property* in the crude sense of today's so-called property rights advocates. The fields and the work pull Jack into a relationship with those who came before and those who will follow:

The work satisfied something deeper in him than his own desire. It was as if he went to his fields in the spring, not just because *he* wanted to, but because his father and grandfather before him had gone because they wanted to—because since the first seeds were planted by hand in the ground, his kinsmen had gone each spring to the fields . . . He remembers those days for their order, the comeliness of the shape his work made in each one of them as it passed. It was an order that came of the union in him of skill and passion, the energy that would not be greater in him than it was then. (Berry 1974, 30)

HOME IS A BASE FOR CONTROL AND POWER

"I'll say when it's quittin' time!"

The famous opening lines to *Gone with the Wind* remind me of the so-called intransigence of older people to change in their home environment. For adult children trying to remove the ubiquitous throw rug at the base of Grandma's stairs, the scene is familiar. What is really at stake is not Grandma's physical safety but who gets to decide. Home, by definition, is a place where "you are in control." Here is how one of Jaber Gubrium's interviewees, Lily Robinson, put it, discussing hospitals and nursing homes:

> I think they all seem about just alike. I stayed in the hospital quite a long time when they amputated my legs and the nurses are friendly, but it's not like home. No place, no hospital, no nursing home is like your own home, not to me. . . . Peace of mind I think at home makes you different. You run your home. These people here run the nursing home. At home, you're the overseer. You take care of everything and I think that's more like a whole being. Here you're just a part. When you're home, you're whole. You're a whole person. You're taking care of everything and everything comes to you by your means and it makes you feel more at home. (1993, 128–29)

Home, it seems, is not merely about brute control, but about human agency, a sense that what you are doing in the world makes a difference that nobody else could make. Anthropologist Michael Jackson, describing the aboriginal Warlpiri of central Australia, describes this sense of agency that accompanies the infusion of material objects with human energy and creativity:

> my experience at the business camp (a kind of men's ceremonial center) reinforced my conviction that a sense of home is grounded less in a place per se than in the activity that goes on in a place. Whether the body is engaged in dancing or in mundane labor, concentrated activity is experienced as a quickened relationship between oneself and whatever one works upon. Inert matter—the ground under one's feet, the shield or spear one fashions—becomes infused with the energy

> and effort that goes into the work. The object comes to
> embody the life of the worker. This means that before the
> Warlpiri recognize a metaphorical fusion between person and
> place, this fusion is felt in bodily praxis. . . . it is the stepping
> up and concentration of activity during ceremony that lends
> a site the depth and density that makes it "sacred." As if the
> earth at that place were stamped and impregnated with the
> vital force of the activities carried out upon it. (1995, 148)

The "householder," nevertheless, does stand within a position of power. He or she is authorized to represent the household to the outside world, as in the U.S. census for example. When you are in my house, you are on my turf. I maintain the power of consent, deciding who shall enter and who shall remain on the outside, a power lost by residents of institutions. As a "homemaker" I decide on an aesthetic for the home. I decide where furniture shall sit. I determine what I will do within—when to eat, when to sleep, when to come and go. Now, it stands to reason, of course, that power within a multiperson household may require negotiation. It may take years to accede to power and only occur with the fall of a matriarch or patriarch. It is gendered. With time and frailty, it may diminish. In the face of threat, the striving for control may take on an urgency that others see as irrational. The "control center" itself, within the home, may retract in scale and, in the end, be manifest merely in a lounge chair and television remote, a tray table by the bed.

Opal, a widow in the Evergreen study, is described by one of the ethnographers:

> Due to her diabetic condition, Opal has begun to lose her
> vision. She is also disabled by the deterioration of cartilage
> in her knees and must now get around with the aid of a
> walker. Opal stays connected to people and the outside world
> through her telephone, cassette tapes, and a radio which are
> all within arm's reach of her easy chair where she sits. She
> keeps phone numbers of neighbors and friends printed in large
> black letters on cards filed by the side of her chair. At night,
> Opal drags her small table, that by day rests next to her easy
> chair, into her bedroom. With it, she takes her telephone
> and radio so that while she lies in bed she can keep in contact
> with friends and listen to the world and Christian news.
> (Unpublished fieldnotes 1995)

Adapting the home to accommodate frailty is one strategy. At the same time, adapting the home to continue to *challenge* one's capacity is equally valuable.

> Naomi explains that she challenges herself to do one thing each day. This may be going to teach Bible study, attending the basketball game of a young member of her church, or just reading. She has also extended the challenge to the minute details of her physical existence, such as consciously deciding not to use the ejector function on her chair or making the effort not to stoop when she walks, even though she has the impulse to look where she is putting her feet. . . . [While] she makes getting around easier by removing throw rugs and placing furniture to provide intermittent resting places as she moves through the house, she also places her everyday china "just out of reach" to promote her own range of motion. Wisely, she puts the plastic items even higher, knowing she may drop an item from time to time. (Fieldnotes 1995)

For the Warlpiri, as for Jack Beechum, this connectedness between body and place, *is* the meaning of home:

> the meaning of home cannot be sought in the substantive, though it may find expression in substantive things like land, house, and family. Experientially, home was a matter of being-at-home-in-the-world. It connoted a sense of existential control and connectedness—the way we feel when what we say or do seems to matter, and there is a balanced reciprocity between the world beyond us and the world within which we move. (Jackson 1995, 154)

THE RHYTHM OF HOME AND AWAY

Several years ago, my good friends Jody Curley, Julie Hill, and their colleagues (my young daughters, Libby and Abby) exercised their talent and creativity to bring about a climate of community among a diverse array of elders with dementia. The day center exhibited the usual supports required and the amenities enjoyed by a wonderful and deserving group of very elderly individuals, along with a special magic, likely engendered by the unconditional respect and appreciation of the staff and volunteers for the participants. Jody and Julie realized the simple truth that two heads are better than one and tapped the collective potential of the community to produce wonderful works of song, art, and phrase. Among the many academic treatises offered to describe the meaning of home, the following poem authored by a small group of elders with dementia expresses, for me, an essential truth:

> I have several homes
> I know a home is a home when I can
> Go there
> Stay
> And go out again
>
> Home is where the dog goes
> When it gets too cold to roam
> When winter's coming on
> That's when I want to go
> Home

As Gary Snyder might say, home is defined by the path.

> The landscape of childhood is learned on foot, and a map is inscribed in the mind—trails, and pathway and grooves—the mean dog, the cranky old man's house, the pasture with a bull in it—going out wider and farther. All of us carry a picture of the terrain that was learned roughly between the ages of six and nine. (It could as easily be an urban neighborhood as some rural scene.) Revisualising that place with its smells and textures, walking through it again in your imagination, has a grounding and settling effect. (1990, 26)

The zen-like equivalence established between going out and coming in, the metaphor of the path, struck home one time in lines spoken by Max, an elder with dementia whom we all loved dearly. When he left the center, a genuine sadness overtook me as I said my good-byes to Max on his last day. We had come to admire and love Max for his unending gentlemanliness and integrity. As a creative and productive electrical engineer, Max had patented many inventions for his company, helping his boss become one of the true early pioneers in the fledgling television industry of the 1950s. At Adult Day Care his identity as an engineer was sustained rigidly in the face of increasing dementia through a constant reference to himself, his peers, and his company, in the corpus of a pictorial history of the company authored by a local industrial historian. This dog-eared book was Max's constant companion and provided ready access to Max's past and present. It would trivialize the importance of the book to say that it merely represented Max's former self. Indeed, the book became Max and Max the book, for whenever the book was out of sight, Max was "out of mind."

Alas, the tribulation of supporting Max at home, with his wandering becoming unmanageable, meant that he would leave Adult Day Care to enter a nursing home. In his inimitable way, Max was taking care of *us* on his last day as we said good-bye; albeit, I grant he did not know what was in store for him. His words had a prophetic Zen-like quality. "We'll be around as long as we can be," he said to me.

Now, as Max wanders the halls of the nursing home, I think perhaps there is a secondary reading of that phrase, which I take to be "We'll be, as long as we're around." *Being around, going around . . .*; that is the primal character of Max's life now, and I see his behavior as a kind of Ur form for us all with its metaphor of the journey as a going and a coming home. As Michael Jackson might describe the peripatetic home-life of the aboriginal Warlpiri of central Australia, existence is defined by the path, the track of dreaming:

> It got me thinking about the motif of the journey, which crops up again and again in Warlpiri myth: the dialectic of coming out . . . and going back in . . . , . . . which at once suggests the passage from birth to death, from day to night, from waking to sleep. (1995, 134)

As the family dog circles the rug, homing in on the center, so we, in our lives, create home not by simply *staying put* but by going out and coming back. In his book of essays by the same title, *Staying Put*, Scott Russell Sanders draws another useful analogy:

> In baseball, home plate is where you begin your journey, and also your destination. You venture out onto the bases, to first and second and third, always striving to return to the spot from which you began. There is danger on the basepath— pick-offs, rundowns, force-outs, double plays—and safety only back at home. I am not saying, as a true fan would, that

baseball is the key to life; rather, life is the key to baseball.
We play or watch this game because it draws pictures of our
desires. (1993, 33)

Despite the static picture of life within, the nursing home itself demonstrates the rhythms we are talking about, though they are typically
unacknowledged for their role in creating home. There *is* home as
defined by the path, spoken by residents outside and inside the nursing
home in interviews in Bloomington and with Jaber Gubrium in *Speaking
of Life*.

Lilian, residing on the "outside," speaks fondly of the fact that her
home is next door to that of her daughter. "There's a path between our
houses," produced by the daily trek of her grandchildren seeking after-
school cookies.

Ruby Coplin, residing "inside," speaks to Gubrium about her life of
giving to others in return for what she herself has been blessed:

> . . . a very close friend. She's Madeline . . . she wasn't bad when
> I first came in and I am very close to her. I feel that God has
> put her in my path, you know, to kind of look after her. And
> then there was Mrs. Edison here . . . we'd wheel her to and
> from the dining room. If she was cold, we'd go get her sweat-
> ers. And then she died. When she left, she had a lot of nice
> things. [After she died] I walked in [her room] . . . this nice
> gentleman comes up and says to me, "I want to shake your
> hand." He said . . ."you're the most wonderful person I've ever
> known . . . the way you were with my mother." She was two
> doors down from me and . . . I kind of adopted her as my
> family. (Gubrium 1993, 52)

For Lilian and Ruby the path expresses their participation in a valued
chain of familial (if fictive) relationships. For others, the image of the
path can be taken more literally. Several times a day, and often late at
night, Etta (on the "inside") makes a cautious but determined trip to
the canteen, one floor down the elevator from her room. There, over
cigarettes and coffee, she meets up with her regular gang to chat, laugh,
reminisce, and talk about what is going on, both inside and outside.
When asked what her definition of home would be, she replies, "I guess
a place where I can go." Her room is sparsely detailed. It is the place
where she goes to rest, between visits to the canteen. Home is the path.

BEING AND DWELLING IN OLD AGE

In poems that honor love and marriage, Wendell Berry often notes how, as dwelling in another, we inhabit a landscape possessed of all the mysteries and beauties we come to know in the forest, the field, the pasture, the town. As Michael Jackson puts it, "The human body and the body of the land share a common language. Person and place coalesce. Whatever happens to the one, happens to the other" (1995, 125). Among philosophers, Martin Heidegger has spoken extensively about the identification of self and place, of dwelling and thinking. He notes that the etymological history of the word dwelling, *bauen*, in German, means to build, but has as its cognate the word *bin*, as in *ich bin*, I am, *du bist*, you are, the imperative form *bis*, to be:

> What then does *ich bin* mean? The old word *bauen*, to which the bin belongs, answers: *ich bin, du bist* mean: I dwell, you dwell. The way in which you are and I am, the manner in which we humans are on the earth, is *Buan*, dwelling. To be human ... means to dwell. (1971, 147)

Yet, Heidegger misses the possibility of home as path. He proceeds to elaborate on the old definition of home to mean *to remain, to stay in a place*. He compares it with the Old Saxon *woun*, which also means to be at peace. Hence, the word "home" comes to mean retreat, a place of safety and security—dwelling as a noun, not a verb. But, as Michael Jackson notes, Heidegger's identification of house and building with self belies a Eurocentric bias emergent with the rise of middle-class, propertied values in the seventeenth century. Prior to that, he explains, citing John Berger, the notion of home connoted village, a group of kin, a state of being (1995, 86). As Dorothy and David Counts (2001) have shown in the wonderful ethnography of older "RV'rs," being on the road is not antithetical to the creation of home. Perhaps the modern version of the peripatetic Warlpiri, older RV'rs pursue the widest possible path, sometimes from Canada to Mexico, a trail of dreaming in which sacred touchstones are visited again and again over years and in which durable friendships are established and reignited as paths cross on an annual basis.

If being and dwelling are identities, and if home and travel are not antithetical, it follows that achieving a sense of place in old age does not require "aging in place," in its narrow sense of aging in the house. Aging with a sense of place can be accomplished in many ways.

The question is not whether staying put or relocating south is the right solution. The question is ... can we fill our spaces with meaning and memory? Can we attain a sense of agency, where what we do makes a difference? Can we dwell in the other? Can we transform space into a place that reflects who we imagine ourselves to be? These are the questions that guide this work. In further chapters we will explore the means and the methods by which individuals and groups can achieve a sense of place in late life, indeed, across the lifespan, for the questions are ageless, the answers important to all generations.

CHAPTER 2

Locating Old Age

The geographer Yi-fu Tuan introduced to us the helpful notion that space and place are codependent but not equivalent concepts (1977). Space, he argued, is defined by a set of locational parameters. Any spot on the earth, of course, can be situated spatially with reference to standard points of reference. Place, on the other hand, comes about when space is infused with meaning. As Yi-fu put it, space becomes place when it partakes of the qualities of the "unplanned human encounter" (1977, 143).

As I write, I sit at the intersection of 39 degrees and 8 minutes north latitude and 86 degrees and 37 minutes west longitude. This defines my space in the world, but it certainly does not describe the place of my existence. This chapter is about the *space* of aging in America, about aging as a locational phenomenon. As a working concept in gerontology, the phrase "aging in place" has typically been taken in its most literal sense, as staying put in one's dwelling unit (e.g., Lanspery and Hyde 1997). Yet, despite being hailed as the pinnacle goal for public policy, there has been a curious lack of serious attention to the deep meaning of place in the lives of elders. As Kevin McHugh and Robert Mings (1996) have noted, much research has been organized around the assumption that there are two basic dichotomous decisions about location in old age—move or stay put (aging in place vs. migration). As a study variable, in short, gerontology has typically focused on space (location) rather than place.

A gerontology of *space* would explore the physical distribution of older people across the landscape. It not only would ask "where do older people live?" but also address the dynamic elements of space—the movement or flow of older people within the environment over time. The same questions are pertinent whether the scope is macro, focusing on entire populations of older people across the entire world, or micro, focusing on the spatial distribution and movement of older people within a single community or even a single neighborhood. In accounting for this distribution, likewise, we should address both the structural and economic forces that push and pull populations across space, as well as the individual decision making that underlies any one person's choice to move (or not) from one place to another, whether in the course of a day or a lifetime.

While we might seek to explain population trends through the lens of political economy, the trends are, in the end, the aggregate of a series of individual decisions, embedded in and emergent from the world of everyday experience, albeit subject to economic forces. A comprehensive, explanatory model should be able to link the two ends of the spectrum, demonstrating how broad trends are the consequence of individual behaviors and, in the process, enable us to address both space *and* place.

Where people live in retirement is, of course, of great popular interest, if one takes the supermarket magazines as an accurate gauge of trends. It is also true, however, that there has been a long-standing academic interest in aging and migration within the field of gerontology. If one were also to infer from the supermarket magazines that "everyone is doin' it—moving to the sun," the academic researchers would quickly point out the errors in this thinking. Despite the broad marketing pitches about retirement migration, older people are less likely to move than any other age group. As the demographers William Haas and William Serow (2002) have noted, on an annual basis only 5 percent of the 65+ population will change residences, compared to much higher rates for other adult age groups. So the quick answer to the question "where do most old people live?" is "where they lived last year."

WHERE OLD PEOPLE LIVED LAST YEAR

University of Michigan demographer William H. Frey clarifies the important distinction between "senior share" and "senior growth" of the population (2006, 21). A quick glance at a map of aging demographics would reveal that the Great Plains, rust belt, and New England show the highest percentages of persons 65+. Pennsylvania, for example, has the third highest percentage of 65+, at over 15 percent. The exception is Florida, of course, with nearly 18 percent of its population falling into this age group. The big states, not surprisingly, contain large numbers of persons 65+, with California at 4 million, Florida at 3 million, New York and Texas each with 2.5 million, and Pennsylvania, Ohio, Illinois, Michigan, New Jersey, and North Carolina each with more than 1 million. These ten states account for 20 million of the 38 million persons over 65 in the United States.

Looking at the growth, not the share, of senior populations over the past two decades reveals a starkly different picture. The differences between Florida and Pennsylvania reflect the distinction that Frey makes. Pennsylvania has a large senior population percentage not because of the growth in this population, but because it has seen years of out-migration and decline in younger age groups, while Florida, of course, has seen a steady influx of seniors. Pennsylvania, in fact, ranks number 50 in the 2000–2010 growth rate of 65+ population, at 2 percent (Frey 2006, 21)! Looking at a map of the growth of the 65+ population moves our eyes from the north to the west and the southeast. As Frey notes, Alaska and Nevada will have increased their senior populations by more than 50 percent by the end of the decade. Other western states with more than a 25 percent growth are Arizona, New Mexico, and Wyoming, followed by the southern states of Texas, Virginia, Georgia, and South Carolina.

If one turns attention to the pre-senior population now entering the 65+ years (the Baby Boomers), a new chapter of the story begins. Twice as large as the current cohort of 65+ seniors, this huge group of emerging seniors would likely have a significant impact on the geography of aging, should it choose to move. However, Frey presents a compelling case that the fastest senior growth trend in the country will be due to "aging in place" and not relocation. In short, Boomers have already moved to the areas in which they are likely to grow old and, for the most part, they are the suburbs. With the 2000 Census, the picture of the suburb as dominated by children and young families was radically revised. More than half of the residents in the suburbs of major metropolitan areas are now age 35 and older and the 1990–2000 growth rate of this population, for the suburbs, nearly doubled that of central cities. Boomers accounted for 31 percent of the total suburban population in 2000. In short, Boomers were not only raised in the suburbs, but they continue to drive suburban growth, especially in the new sunbelt and New West metro areas such as Las Vegas, El Paso, Austin, Phoenix-Mesa, Colorado Springs, and Atlanta. From 1990 to 2000, the percentage change in the 35+ population in these suburban areas ranged from 56 percent to 90 percent (Frey 2003, 9). While the Boomer populations in the suburbs of older metro areas such as Chicago, Pittsburgh, Dayton, etc., will have an impact as they age in place, these areas were less likely to experience the earlier growth as Boomers moved south and west. Frey distinguishes between suburbs with the more recent fastest senior growth and those "senior suburban havens" that were settled earlier and now see high senior shares (Sarasota-Bradenton, West Palm Beach–Boca Raton, Tampa–St. Petersburg, Scranton-Hazelton, and Pittsburgh). Overall, as Frey argues, the effect of aging in place of the current Boomers will far outweigh net migration as a driver of future senior growth (2007, 13).

WHERE OLD PEOPLE WILL MOVE

While the percentage of the population that moves in retirement is relatively small, the absolute numbers support a huge retirement housing industry. Also, the number of people relocating in retirement can certainly have an impact on the communities and regions that find themselves on both the sending and the receiving ends of the migration phenomenon. This impact has spurred Pennsylvania to create a special program to slow the out-migration of older Pennsylvanians (and their portfolios), just as sunbelt communities, and even entire states, have created programs to attract retirees (and their portfolios).

William Walters (2002) suggests that research on retirement migration has been organized around two conceptual models, the push-pull model and the life-course model. As the name suggests, the push-pull model tries to identify attractive and unattractive features of places that encourage and/or discourage in-migration and out-migration. The complementary life-course model looks at the personal attributes and characteristics of actual and potential migrants across the life course.

LIFE-COURSE ATTRIBUTES

As a step toward segmenting the population of migrants (in later life), Walters selected three primary, measurable attributes of migrating individuals in later life: economic status, disability status, and presence or absence of a spouse (2002, 268ff). Conflating these attributes with household characteristics of migrants (residential independence, economic independence, institutionalization, and housing cost) and with direction of migration (in or out) enabled the sorting of migrants into three identifiable types, the members of each type being similar in their life-course attributes, their spatial pattern of migration, and their household characteristics.

- *Amenity-seeking migrants* are typically, but not necessarily, healthy, married, and financially secure. They constitute the largest segment of migrants (46 percent) and, as the definition would suggest, seek communities with particular appealing amenities (discussed below).

- *Assistance-seeking migrants* (28 percent of Walters's sample) are characterized by a greater degree of residential and economic dependence; that is, they are more likely unmarried and dependent on others (especially family) for income and housing. Unlike the amenity-seeking migrants, Walters found no coherent pattern in the destinations sought by assistance-seeking migrants.

- *Migrants with severe disabilities* (26 percent) are individuals at all income levels who move in response to the development of a severe disability. In most cases, the move involves relocation to a nursing home (40 percent of the group) or adult child residence.

In addition to describing the background characteristics of the migrant groups, researchers have investigated the decision-making processes that underlie the choice to move. Charles Longino and colleagues (2002) reviews some of the personal elements involved in relocation decisions. Citing the work of L. J. Cuba and D. M. Hummon (1993a; 1993b), he notes that making a move to a new environment challenges one's sense of "place identity," a well of meaning derived from the personal memories and symbolic significance associated with place. In addition, "staying in a familiar pre-retirement location promises an environment where retirees understand the rhythms and routines of life." One could surmise from this assertion that individuals who have made multiple moves over the course of a lifetime might be predisposed to engage in additional moves in retirement and be less dependent on place for a sense of identity. Indeed, their identity (and their adaptive skill) is tied to "traveling," a term taken from the work of Jaber Gubrium (1993, 103ff). This argument is strengthened, Longino would suggest, when we incorporate the evidence that vacation and tourism patterns predict retirement destination choices. In addition, relocation decisions are often based on existing ties to friends and family in the destination communities, as McHugh and Mings demonstrate. And, of course, snowbirds often develop steadily lengthening relationships with seasonal destinations that may resolve into permanent residence. Stephen Katz (2005) provides a rich descrip-tion of the chain migration patterns of Canadians to Florida and the creation of enclaves that, to a degree, replicate home communities in a warm weather setting.

PLACES THAT PUSH/PLACES THAT PULL

Walters's review of the migration literature (including popular retirement guides) identified nearly 300 place characteristics that might be implicated in decisions to move or to stay put. From this comprehensive list, he selected 24 items, based on their pertinence to the hypotheses being tested and their clean "measurability." The study confirms the importance of climate in the destination community as the most significant predictor of in-migration for amenity-seeking retirees, a finding echoed by Longino. Longino notes as well, however, that climate preferences can work both ways. Older Minnesotans moving to Florida will most frequently mention the warm climate as a pull factor, while those northerners staying put some-times view "the changing seasons" as a factor in the decision to stay.

Walters and others have begun to articulate a more refined definition of the role that the natural environment plays in retirement relocation deci-sions. In the study cited above, Walters identifies a subset of environmental factors that play a role in the destination choice of amenity-seeking migrants: winter mildness; summer air moisture; winter air moisture; summer temperature mildness; wind speed and fog; lake/ocean access. Among all of the variables, he concludes that winter mildness (moderate temperature and low snowfall) is the single most important predictor. Scott Wright, Michael Caserta, and Dale Lund (2003) would add "scenic beauty" to the list of environmental factors cited by amenity-seeking migrants to the New West (see below) and note the related environmental aspects of recreational pursuits sought by migrants (skiing, hiking, boating, etc.).

In addition to the natural environment as a factor in decision making, a number of other place characteristics have been implicated. In his list of variables, Walters added:

- *Population and population density*: Amenity-seeking retirees are inclined to avoid large metropolitan areas and seem to prefer smaller cities and towns. Areas with high concentrations of retirees seem to attract more retirees. For retirees living in high population density areas, out-migration is deterred, however, perhaps a factor of rent-controlled housing costs. Retirees living in large metropolitan areas can often find amenities through a local move, while retirees in smaller towns may be more likely to require a longer distance move to reach preferred amenities.

- *Economic indices:* Using employment figures as an index of community economic health and prosperity, Walters suggests prosperous communities are more likely to support recreational and cultural amenities.
- *Medical care:* The availability of long-term care beds, more so than hospital beds, is a strong predictor for those with severe disabilities. Sufficient local availability deters out-migration and becomes an attractive characteristic in destination communities for this subgroup. Insufficient local availability of long-term care beds is a predictor of out-migration among assistance-seeking migrants. The presence of adult children in the destination community is a major consideration for assistance-seeking migrants, though this introduces randomness into the model for adult children live everywhere, so to speak.
- *Crime rates:* High crime rates appear to be associated with local migration but are not a factor in interstate migration.

A brief review of the nonscientific "retirement living guides" suggests that other place characteristics touted to amenity-seeking migrants include cost of living, cultural amenities, community ambience, and the service environment (libraries, wellness facilities, access to transportation).

RETIRING TO THE NEW WEST

When looking at more recent retirement migration trends, one might also surmise that the Sun City stereotype is being challenged. It appears that increasing numbers of retirees are exploring new territory and rejecting the gated Sun City model. One 2007 retirement guide includes three non-sunbelt communities in its list of the top five retirement communities. While climate might still be argued to be a predominant feature of migration decisions, it is clear that retirement to Telluride is not the same as retirement to Tucson.

J. Matthew Shumway and Samuel M. Otterstrom (2001) provide a fascinating review of the significant demographic trends that have transformed the Old West into the New West. Noting how worldwide competition has led to a decline in extractive industries (mining, ranching, farming, logging), the authors discuss the concomitant job growth related to environmental amenities, specifically tourism, second homes, and retire-ment (service-related industries). They suggest that a fundamental shift in the economy has occurred, involving not the exploitation of natural resour-ces, but the exploitation of the natural environment as a place. Interest-ingly, they note that these quality of life factors contribute to population growth (both through in-migration and dampening of out-migration), with jobs following the growth, rather than the other way around. To demon-strate their argument, the authors developed a typology of counties in the West, including both dominant economic characteristics and an "amenity index." Of 246 rural counties in the western states, 76 were classified as New West, differentiated statistically with the highest natural amenity index, the highest amount of service-related employment, the highest amount of federal land ownership, and are major retirement and recreation destinations. New growth has concentrated in these New West counties, often characterized by a somewhat developed infrastructure and extant rec-reational and scenic amenities. The most intense clustering has occurred in western Colorado, southern Wyoming, and northern New Mexico, where famous destinations and attractions are also in close proximity to metropoli-tan areas. During the 1990s the rural Mountain West grew by 700,000 people and, amazingly, 70 percent of rural counties experienced net in-migration.

As Wright et al. note, aging is a major driver of these population and economic changes in the West. Citing U.S. Census figures, they note that between 1990 and 2000, the western region of the United States experi-enced the highest increase (20 percent) in the 65 and older population, with Nevada's older population growing 72 percent and with Las Vegas as the metropolitan area with the greatest increase (65 percent) among all metro areas in the country.

Policy makers, citizens, and researchers have been increasingly concerned about the environmental impacts of retirement migration to the New West. In their investigation of elders' attitudes toward protec-tion of the natural environment in Utah, Wright et al. observed a diverse set of orientations. A generally positive attitude toward protection of the environment masked a good deal of underlying diversity as to how it should be done. Certain segments of the retirement population main-tained a conservative skepticism regarding the role of the govern-ment, preferring the role be left to industry and the business community. They exhibited a strong distrust of national environmental

groups. Other segments were vocal in their support for stronger protec-
tions and more liberal in their approach to environmental issues. Interestingly, the former attitudes were more likely to be evinced by long-
term residents, the latter by "newcomers," who tended to be younger in
age as well and more heterogeneous in their religious affiliation (less
likely to be members in the Church of Latter-day Saints). The authors
note that the former group may also be more likely to benefit from the
economic development in retirement "hot spots" and, hence, less
inclined to support growth limits. The diversity in perspectives represents
an interesting echo of the more general tensions arising in the New West
around environmental issues. They suggest that the growing number of
Baby Boomers in the West will add to the heated debate. Insofar as a
growing proportion of Baby Boomers seek civic engagement as well, the
potential for a more collaborative conservation movement (balancing
local and federal interests) may be enhanced.

COLLEGE TOWNS

In another challenge to the Sun City model, an increasing number of
retirement migrants are finding their way to college towns. *The New York
Times* reported there are more than 50 retirement communities located
on or near college campuses in the United States (2007). The communities exhibit many of the pull characteristics identified in Walters's list:
healthier local economies that can support a richer service environment;
lower crime rates; quality health care systems, including teaching hospitals; and, of course, a rich array of low-cost recreational, cultural, and
educational amenities. These amenities can outweigh the role of climate
in retirement decision making and, as a consequence, many college towns
throughout the country have begun concerted efforts to attract retirees.
The small city of Columbia, Missouri, certainly not sunbelt, initiated a
Retire to Columbia campaign in 1994, advertising in multiple national
publications and generating a movement that had attracted an estimated
2,700 new migrants to the city by the year 2000. Other college towns
have followed suit and now aggressively market their amenities to Baby
Boomers and new retirees.

RETIRING TO THE CITY

While not a mass movement, there is some irony in the reverse movement of Boomers from the suburbs to the cities. In a white paper for the

Living Cities Census Series, Eugenie C. Birch (2005) has reviewed the recent demographics of downtown revitalization efforts nationwide. She notes that residential development has become one of the linchpins of downtown revival strategies. "Many downtowns boast a large number of assets that support residential uses. Architecturally interesting build-ings, waterfront property, a rich cultural heritage, bustling entertainment sectors, specialized services like healthcare and higher education, and, of course, proximity to jobs are common attributes" (Birch 2005, 2). As one might infer from the retirement migration research, cities will have strong appeal for amenity-seeking Baby Boomers. While the growth remains relatively modest, downtown housing is on the upswing and Baby Boomers are, it appears, helping to fuel the trend. While young adults lead the march, Baby Boomers (especially empty nesters and single-person households) are not far behind. In the year 2000, the age group 45–64 comprised 21 percent of the downtown population, a figure that Birch suggests will continue to grow in the future.

WILL BABY BOOMERS SEEK SUN CITY?

Haas and Serow have raised a number of provocative questions about whether the Baby Boom generation will follow the same patterns of retirement migration as the current generation or bring an end to the Golden Age of retirement communities. As the previously cited research on migration attests, amenity-seeking retirement has traditionally been based on a clean break with work life and enabled by a solid economic footing. Haas and Serow suggest that there are signs of change on the Boomer horizon, which might signal new forms of retirement and affect the migration model.

The Timing of Retirement

For most of the twentieth century, age at retirement exhibited a con-tinuous decline, enabled by improving pension benefits and the availabil-ity of social security at age 62. By 1985, the average age of retirement had reached 60 and only 18 percent of the age 65–69 population was in the workforce (Gist 2007). This trend certainly helped fuel the creation of the "golden years" model of a leisure-filled retirement.

Now it appears the trend has reversed itself. Average age of retirement has lengthened from age 60 to age 62. Of the 60+ population, 29 percent are working (Gist). AARP reports that 80 percent of the Boomers expect to work at least part time in retirement and one in four Boomers report they plan to never retire!

For the individual worker, however, age at retirement is not always driven by choice. Often, it is driven by need, due to changes in health status or company downturns. When evaluating the prospective retirement ages of Boomers, however, we cannot predict these changes. Hence, speculation on when Boomers will retire is based on their reported expectations, which sometimes do not come to pass. Nevertheless, there is strong evidence that Boomers will spend more years in the workforce than their predecessors. Social policy makers are thrilled at the prospect, since this will generate tax revenues to help offset the significant pressure on the system over the next 30 years.

Gordon Mermin, Richard Johnson, and Dan Murphy (2007) suggest that this likelihood of continued employment might be driven by negative factors, i.e., the erosion of traditional defined benefit plans and employer-sponsored health benefits. Of course, changes in Social Security policy itself also incentivize later retirement. Boomers will be eligible at age 66, not 65, and the reduction in benefits for early retirement is being increased.

When looking at Boomer expectations, moreover, there is clear evidence of changing attitudes. Haas and Serow note that Boomers are less likely than current retirees to have followed a traditional career path. Such individuals are more likely to reenter the workforce in postretirement. Similarly, higher educational levels increase the likelihood of continued engagement with the workforce, albeit in consulting capacities or in a part-time capacity. Increasingly, Boomers are engaging in entrepreneurial activity, abandoning their traditional careers and starting up new businesses (Karoly and Zissimopoulos 2004). Many women in the Boomer generation have been strongly career oriented, unlike their mothers and grandmothers and, hence, more likely to stay engaged with work. As Haas and Serow note, it is from the ranks of the more economically independent early retirees that the age-dense active retirement communities have been filled. The longer Boomers work, the less likely they are to spend their "active years" in Sun City.

Financing Retirement

Aside from the leisure time created through early retirements, the Sun City lifestyle has depended on the solid financial footing of the current cohort, itself a factor of the savings habits of the current elder generation and the successes of organized labor in improving the financial status of retirees. As mentioned above, the erosion of defined benefit pension plans creates a level of uncertainty regarding the economic well-being of the next generation of retirees. Haas and Serow note that defined contribution plans and the more recently popular individual retirement accounts and other annuity-like vehicles depend for their down-the-road value on the performance of equity markets and, as such, are more volatile than the traditional plans of the current generation of retirees. The availability of early withdrawal might also tempt retirees to cash out too early, thus jeopardizing the long-term financing of a retirement lifestyle.

When it comes to savings, American households have exhibited a continuous decline, from 10 percent in the 1950s to 3 percent by the mid-1990s (Moore and Mitchell 1997). While Baby Boomers as a whole are expected to be wealthier than their parents, important subgroups will be doing worse and, relative to the continuation of preretirement lifestyles, Boomers may fare worse given inflationary factors (Butrica, Iams, and Smith 2003). On the positive side, risks associated with lower accumulation of wealth among Boomers might be offset by the potentially huge intergenerational transfer of wealth from the World War II (WWII) generation to the Boomers, an amount that might reach $1 trillion (Haas and Serow 2002, 158). Annamaria Lusardi and Olivia Mitchell (2007) report that wealth accumulation for Boomers equals that of their parents but that, again, important subgroups, particularly those who do not plan for retirement, may find themselves facing retirement with very little or no wealth.

Boomer Households and Lifestyles

Another factor likely to influence the character of retirement migration is the nature of the Boomer household itself. Hakan Aykan (2003) notes that lower (and likely later) rates of marriage and higher rates of divorce have combined to lower fertility levels among the Baby Boom generation, as compared to the WWII generation, potentially leading to historically low levels of childlessness. Insofar as decisions to migrate, especially with the onset of dependency, are driven by family concerns, it might be reasoned that a greater number of Boomers will be "footloose," without adult children or grandchildren to either provide or receive care.

Given the unknowns regarding the timing and financing of retirement, the changing character of households among the Baby Boom generation, and the changing locational preferences Boomers have already exhibited, it is arguable that the Sun City real estate ventures of the past may not reap the benefits that the population surge itself would promise. Indeed, the most significant changes in the elderscape to come will not come from relocation but from the prospect that Boomers will, in the end, follow their parents' path and choose to "age in place."

✌ JEWEL'S STUFF ✍

As a resident of a local nursing home, Jewel lives with and among her things. Despite the constricted space, one finds a veritable storehouse of knickknacks, crafty things, Teddy bears, clothing on hangers, bottles, and party leftovers. She knows that she is pushing the official limit on this issue. "Some think it's junk, and I know it's tacky, but it's my junk," she explains. As we do a tape-recorded inventory of each and every object (really a task beyond the scope of my capability as a fieldworker with limited time), Jewel comments on the significance of each. The history of some objects is lost to memory but usually noted as something that "someone gave to me." Being the recipient of many little gifts has significance for Jewel, though not in any boastful fashion. The handmade afghan at the end of her bed epitomizes the relevance of gifts to her. It had belonged to the woman across the hall and, upon her death, was given by her son to Jewel. "You always smiled at my mother," he said, "and we wanted you to know we appreciated that."

In the corner are stacked two large cardboard boxes, buckling under the weight of additional items piled on top. "In there is my frying pan, and I'll never give that up," Jewel says. I am reminded of my fieldwork visits years ago to Lu McDonald in her tiny, frail little house in Switz City, and the relevance of her frying pan to her: "My house'd burn down, but I'd still have my fryin' pan," was the way she put it. That image of the frying pan, strong as the woman who handles it (or wields it, in the cartoon image), fits Jewel, though to see it one has to look past her southern ladylike gentility bred of a Jackson, Mississippi, upbringing, and past her own frail visage diminished by Parkinson's disease.

CHAPTER 3

The Domains of an Elder-friendly Community

In the Introduction, I argued for a paradigm shift within the fields of gerontology and geriatrics—a shift from a predominant focus on the individual aging body to a focus on the body-in-place, where "place" refers not merely to the physical forces of the environment, but to the meaning-laden lifeworld that we occupy. Such a perspective leads reformers to a new set of questions about aging in America. Instead of asking how it is that individual elders "succeed" at aging, it asks "what are the characteristics of communities that enable elders to flourish?"

This question guided the thoughts of Penny Feldman, Mia Oberlink, and the author as they conceived and proposed a project in 1999 entitled: Benchmarks for Elder-Friendly Communities (Feldman and Oberlink 2003). Feldman was the director of the Center for Home Care Policy and Research at the Visiting Nurse Service of New York, the oldest and largest visiting nurse service in the country. Initial conversations with several private foundations resulted in support for an exploration of the notion of elder-friendly communities with key thought leaders in the field of gerontology. A review of literature found no systematic framework of "indicators" that a community might use to measure its elder-friendliness, though the notion of deriving quality of life and environmental indicators was beginning to take hold in progressive cities around the nation and world. While indicators projects were surfacing to measure fairly broad quality of life elements, we found no clear examples of communities adapting an indicators framework that focused specifically on aging and well-being. Data on this issue at the local level were scarce, though the U.S. Census did provide certain potentially useful key indicators that could be incorporated. "Housing cost burden," the amount of gross income spent on household expenses by age group, for example, is a very useful indicator of welfare and can be used as a community benchmark. Other markers beyond the census, such as health and retirement data, were seen as important, but, being drawn from national sampling surveys, did not provide data that could be used at the local level, as does the census. By and large, the broad range of data required for an adequate representation of the status of older people at the local level was not available. This required the development of a new "indicators" survey instrument that communities could use to assess their elder-friendliness.

The first step in developing such a tool, of course, was to articulate the notion of an elder-friendly community. A focus group strategy was chosen and with the assistance of Axiom Research of Boston, the research team selected four diverse U.S. communities in order to engage directly with elders and community leaders around the subject. Communities visited include Chicago, Illinois, Allentown, Pennsylvania, Raleigh, North Carolina, and Long Beach, California. In each community, telephone lists were retrieved to enable randomized calls to create three panels of elders in each community across a range of age from 45 to 90. In addition, a snowball approach was used to identify and create a panel of community leaders, including municipal officials and leaders outside of the traditional aging network.

In order to engender some creative thinking around this subject, each focus group participant was requested to design and fabricate a collage/poster that would demonstrate their own ideas about what makes a community elder-friendly. The team was delighted with the response. Most participants arrived with posters and were very pleased to share them in the group discussion. (See Chapter 4 for a complete description of this method.) While retirement to golf figured prominently in one younger man's worldview, the majority of participants voiced the common refrain of "aging in place." A systematic review of focus group transcripts, including those of community leaders, revealed four basic and essential "domains of an elder-friendly community," later graphically portrayed in what has come to be known as the circles chart; see Chart 3-1.

Given these broad domains and the implicated dimensions within each circle, the task was set to outline a list of measurable "indicators" and develop questions the summarized responses to which would provide a baseline snapshot of a community's elder-friendliness through the eyes

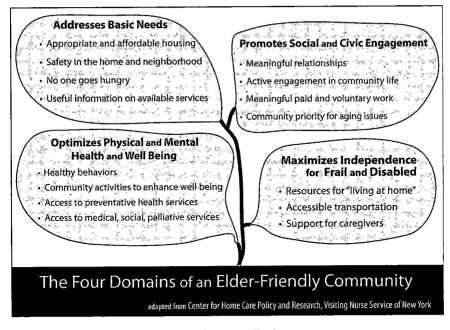

The Four Domains of an Elder-Friendly Community

adapted from Center for Home Care Policy and Research, Visiting Nurse Service of New York

Chart 3-1   The Four Domains of Elder-Friendly Community

[adapted from Center for Home Care Policy and Research, Visiting Nurse Service of New York]

of the older population. Moreover, a survey that could be replicated across a number of communities would provide a comparative framework enabling each community to establish benchmarks and goals for change.

A total of 33 different indicators were selected, as illustrated in Table 3-1.

For each indicator, the team initially sought survey questions that may have already been tested and validated in other national sampling surveys. Using a standard question, if available, would provide yet another basis for comparison with existing research studies. For most indicators, however, a new question needed to be formulated. Working closely with the survey subcontractor, a 25-minute telephone survey instrument, screening protocol, and sampling methodology was developed.

Concomitant to the development of the survey, the research team identified and recruited ten prospective cities and towns to serve as a pilot group for the conducting of the survey and the implementation of a community planning process. We sought some diversity in the collection of communities by size, geography, and population makeup. We also sought communities that exhibited local commitment of leadership and a small contribution of funding. Several communities provided leadership

Table 3-1   Essential Elements of an Elder-Friendly Community

It addresses basic needs.

Affordable housing is available to community residents	1. Percentage of people age 65+ who spend >30%/<30% of their income on housing
	2. Percentage of people age 65+ who want to remain in their current residences and are confident they will be able to afford to do so
Housing is modified to accommodate mobility and safety	3. Percentage of householders age 65+ in housing units with met/ unmet home modification needs
The neighborhood is livable and safe	4. Percentage of people age 65+ who feel safe/unsafe in their neighborhood
	5. Percentage of people age 65+ who report few/multiple problems in the neighborhood
	6. Percentage of people age 65+ who are satisfied with the neighborhood as a place to live
People have enough to eat	7. Percentage of people age 65+ who report cutting the size of or skipping meals due to lack of money
Assistance services are available and residents know how to access them	8. Percentage of people age 65+ who do not know whom to call if they need information about services in their community
	9. Percentage of people age 65+ who are aware/unaware of selected services in their community
	10. Percentage of people age 65+ with adequate assistance in activities of daily living (ADL) and/or instrumental activities of daily living (IADL)

It optimizes physical and mental health and well being.

Community promotes and provides access to necessary and preventive health services	11. Rates of screening and vaccination for various conditions among people 65+
	12. Percentage of people age 65+ who felt depressed or anxious and have not seen a health care professional (for those symptoms)
	13. Percentage of people age 65+ whose physical or mental health interfered with their activities in the past month
	14. Percentage of people age 65+ who report being in good to excellent health
Opportunities for physical activity are available and used	15. Percentage of people age 65+ who participate in regular physical exercise
Obstacles to use of necessary medical care are minimized	16. Percentage of people age 65+ with a usual source of care
	17. Percentage of people age 65+ who failed to obtain needed medical care
	18. Percentage of people age 65+ who had problems paying for medical care
	19. Percentage of people age 65+ who had problems paying for prescription drugs
	20. Percentage of people age 65+ who had problems obtaining dental care or eyeglasses
Palliative care services are available and advertised	21. Percentage of people age 65+ who have used or know how to access palliative care services

It maximizes independence for the frail and persons with disabilities.

Transportation is accessible and affordable	22. Percentage of people age 65+ who have access to public transportation
The community service system enables people to live comfortably and safely at home	23. Percentage of people age 65+ with adequate assistance in ADL
	24. Percentage of people age 65+ with adequate assistance in IADL
Caregivers are mobilized to complement the formal service system	25. Percentage of people age 65+ who provide help to the frail or disabled
	26. Percentage of people age 65+ who get respite/relief from their caregiving activity

It promotes social and civic engagement.

Residents maintain connections with friends and neighbors	27. Percentage of people age 65+ who socialized with friends or neighbors in the past week
Civic, cultural, religious, and recreational activities include older residents	28. Percentage of people age 65+ who attended church, temple, or other in the past week
	29. Percentage of people age 65+ who attended movies, sports events, clubs, or group events in the past week
	30. Percentage of people age 65+ who engaged in at least one social, religious, or cultural activity in the past week
Opportunities for volunteer work are readily available	31. Percentage of people age 65+ who participate in volunteer work
Community residents help and trust each other	32. Percentage of people age 65+ who live in "helping communities"
Appropriate work is available to those who want it	33. Percentage of people age 65+ who would like to be working for pay

through the local agency on aging. In others, primary leadership was provided by a local private foundation or health care system. In the end, we
gathered a group of ten U.S. communities:

- Six neighborhoods of Chicago, Illinois
- Indianapolis, Indiana
- Jacksonville, Florida
- Lincoln Square, New York City
- Maricopa County, Arizona
- Orange County, Florida
- Puyallup, Washington
- Santa Clarita, California
- Upper West Side, New York City
- Yonkers, New York

Working under a new name—the AdvantAge Initiative—the ten
community teams convened for two multiday retreats in New York City.
These training retreats provided an opportunity to orient each community to the proposed survey process and develop local plans for assuring
success in achieving support and participation in the survey and associated planning events. In addition, the meetings helped build enthusiasm
for the work and the expertise needed to carry out local planning and
development projects. Participants learned about participatory research
and community development; about strategic communication and social
marketing; about collaborative leadership and outreach; and about inter-
preting and making use of statistical data from the prospective surveys.
    Over a period of several months in 2000–2001, the initial AdvantAge
Initiative telephone survey was conducted in each of the ten participating communities. A randomized sample of 500 individuals age 65 and
over was achieved in each community, providing a wealth of data that
was then analyzed and portrayed in an extensive data chartbook developed for each. In addition to the results for each of the 33 indicators,
broken down further along several demographic parameters, the group
of ten received a comparison chart for each indicator that provided
companion data for the "highest and lowest" results and an average of
results across all ten communities. Chart 3-2 provides an example of the
overall results for one indicator, for Indianapolis, which would be accompanied by a breakdown for three age groups ("young old to old old"), race,

gender, education, number in household, self-reported health status, activity limitations, and presence of friends in the neighborhood. Chart 3-3 provides an example of the all-community comparison provided to Indianapolis on the selected indicator.

Armed with a mountain of data about the older population, each community proceeded to develop a community-wide collaborative process to "make meaning" from the data and employ them to promote community change. We learned that the data had multiple uses. They could be used to raise awareness about aging issues; to set priorities based on a reading of the data and comparisons with other communities; to design action plans around particular indicators; to undergird decisions by multiple community interests around the allocation of resources; and, ideally, to monitor progress toward goals through remeasuring selected indicators at a later date.

Many of the communities initiated planning activities through convening wide-scale summits or town meetings, including press coverage and attempts to engage with audiences who might not have identified with aging as a key issue or concern. They often included popular keynote speakers and typically involved carefully constructed slide presentations of the local data. Most used these meetings as an opportunity to hook citizens into follow-up planning

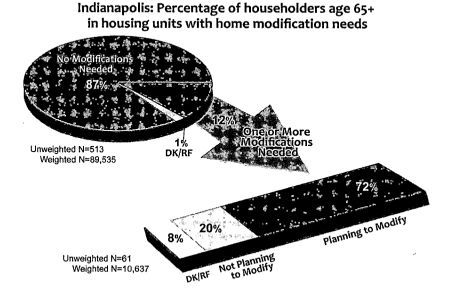

Chart 3-2 User-friendly charts display survey results for individual indicators

All-Community Comparison
Percentage of householders age 65+
in housing units with home modification needs

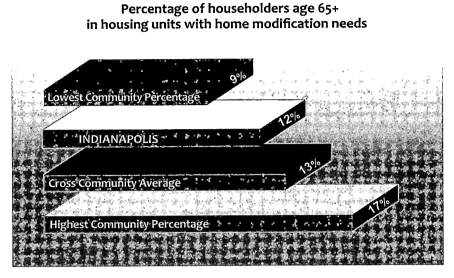

Chart 3-3 Comparison charts enable communities to assess their status vis à vis others in the United States

activities and, in some communities, the meetings themselves involved work by participants to respond to the data and shape issues and priorities. Local publications were developed to summarize the data and publicize planning priorities and actions along the way. David Hanson and Charles Emlet (2006) provide a summary of one community's approach to the project (Puyallup, Washington). Citizen participation evolved as a valued component, and efforts were made to integrate young people into the process. In Puyallup, Washington, the local survey revealed a disturbing lack of familiarity with local aging services among the respondents, which became a priority issue for the planning task force. In developing a marketing strategy to improve awareness, the local team brought together young art students with community elders, who were invited to discuss their beliefs about the essence of the region. These beliefs were artistically interpreted by the students and incorporated as visual elements in a poster campaign about information and referral services. Within one year, the number of calls to the local area agency on aging increased by 250 percent!

In the smallest participating community, the high-rises of Amsterdam Houses in Lincoln Square, Manhattan, the survey revealed an alarming sense of insecurity among these very low income, mostly African American tenants. This provided an opportunity for the local leaders to convene a large community meeting, with special invitations to local police, as well as public housing and elected officials. Many tenants were given an opportunity through their personal stories to explain why rates of insecurity were high in the face of official government crime statistics that suggested otherwise. The local police official was both surprised and a little chagrined to learn that elderly tenants were not likely to report crime when to do so might provoke a loss of privacy and even potential retaliation by perpetrators. The public airing of this data in front of influential legislators and public officials started a change process that continues to this day. Police presence increased. The Public Housing Authority stepped up maintenance and security. Local health care providers began collaborating to provide social work and mental health services to residents. Elected officials assigned staff to regular contact with the project. Survey data informed several successful grant proposals that have enabled weekend meals services and health promotion programs. The U.S. Postal Service itself installed a box on the premises, thus reducing the risks associated with the simple task of mailing a letter, something that most of us take quite for granted.

Numerous other success stories emerged from the national AdvantAge Initiative project during its first few years. Jacksonville, Florida, employed survey data to heavily influence the priority setting process of the local United Way. Winter Park, Florida, employed the data to create community work groups that resulted in a major summit on mobility and a year-long marketing campaign to increase awareness about healthy aging. Yonkers, New York, folded in additional funding from multiple sources to initiate a broad asset-based development process focusing on such issues as civic engagement and leadership development for elders and intergenerational approaches to community-wide issues. From the survey of seniors in Indianapolis, home modification for aging-in-place was identified as a significant need. Outside funding was acquired to address this need as part of a pilot, neighborhood elder-friendliness program. In its first year, 17 homes were modified with ramps, grab bars, widened doorways, and accessible showers. Lilly Pharmaceuticals, which is based in the city, dovetailed that neighborhood program with an army of volunteers for an extraordinary home repair blitz in the summer of 2009.

Not every pilot community could attest to such results, but the AdvantAge Initiative planning model proved both workable and worthwhile.

This success accounted for increasing national interest in the project in subsequent years. In 2004 the Atlantic Philanthropies underwrote the cost of a national sampling survey, which provides yet another scale for comparison with local results. Additional communities found funding to adapt the survey and process to their areas, including Grand Rapids, Michigan, El Paso, Texas, and Contra Costa, California, which won the National Council on the Aging (NCOA) RespectAbility Program award for its achievements.

In 2005, the first statewide application of the AdvantAge Initiative (AI) model was implemented in Indiana, through demonstration funding from the U.S. Administration on Aging (Grant No. 90AM3026). The state unit on aging (within the Family and Social Services Administration) saw this as an opportunity to test the effectiveness of the AI planning model on a statewide basis and its potential application on a nationwide basis. The planning initiative would be comprehensive, data driven, and participatory (Stafford 2006).

As in previous projects, data would be provided by the application of the AI survey, then embedded within a participation process designed to engage new partners, reaching out beyond the traditional aging network to broaden the "ownership" of aging issues in communities throughout the state. During the first two years of the three-year project, additional funding was secured to conduct the survey in a most comprehensive fashion. As before, local community groups were provided support and training to orient to the planning model and develop community partnerships and collaborations in preparation for the survey release.

The survey began in January 2008, and by the end of May a total of 5,000 randomly selected residents age 60 and over had participated in the survey. The total sample included approximately 300 Hoosiers in 15 planning and service areas (PSAs) representing the Area Agencies on Aging (AAAs) and nearly 500 randomly selected older Hoosiers residing in five neighborhood naturally occurring retirement communities (NNORCs). By June, AI staff members were providing extensive reports on all 33 indicators for use by the state unit and by the local PSAs. Each PSA received the raw frequencies for each question on the survey, easily readable pie charts and tables with the demographic analyses, and comparison charts revealing variation in indicator results across the several geographic levels. A project Web site, www.agingindiana.org, was created to serve as a public repository for the data.

By the end of December 2008, nearly every AAA had organized local planning initiatives, ranging in scale from small senior-led neighborhood

NNORC committees, fostered by the University of Indianapolis, to area-wide planning workshops. Seventeen planning workshops were held around the state and typically involved the presentation of survey data for the relevant area, followed by a participatory planning workshop to assist community members in "making meaning from the data" and moving toward action. Technical assistance to the leaders of the local planning initiatives focused on broadening stakeholder participation in the planning process (Stafford 2001). At the close of the three-year project, a Web-based survey of PSA leadership (with 12 of 16 local initiatives responding) demonstrated the following results:

- 100 percent reported that the project has provided a rich amount of data for local, area, and state planning purposes.
- 92 percent agreed or strongly agreed that the planning demonstration engaged new participants at the local and area level in the development of community plans for aging. Groups cited as new participants by more than 50 percent of the respondents included: (1) baby-boomers (75 percent); (2) business leaders (67 percent); (3) elected and professional government officials (75 percent); (4) health care leaders (50 percent).
- 82 percent agreed or strongly agreed that the project resulted in the appearance of new forms of financial and social capital dedicated to the creation of more elder-friendly communities.
- 83 percent agreed or strongly agreed that the project helped facilitate the process of creating an effective and comprehensive area plan on aging.
- 100 percent agreed or strongly agreed that the project helped create an increased presence of aging issues on the public/media agenda.
- 75 percent agreed or strongly agreed that the project resulted in improved decision-making processes for the allocation of resources by public and private funders.
- 36 percent felt that the project elevated individual gift giving to area aging programs.
- 63 percent reported the project has resulted in new public funding allocations.
- 75 percent reported that, as a consequence of the project, new volunteers have joined aging-related programs.

- 54 percent reported seeing changes in public policy that will create positive change toward more elder-friendly communities.
- 70 percent reported seeing new aging-related initiatives in traditionally nonaging related organizations.
- 100 percent agreed or strongly agreed that the project has led to more consistent and clear planning methods across the group of Area Agencies on Aging in Indiana.

In the coming years, the AdvantAge Initiative team will be continuing to explore ways to support citizen planning for elder-friendly communities. Funding from the Daniels Fund in Denver, Colorado, is supporting the development of educational and consulting tools to enable citizens groups to develop action programs around specific indicators and social marketing tools to assist in developing public awareness and cultural change campaigns around key issues that communities wish to address. The evaluation outcomes discussed above will provide a framework for developing new tools to enable communities to improve their local planning through monitoring and assessing their work processes.

SOME OBSERVATIONS ON CHANGE

The world would probably be a better place if we knew what the necessary and sufficient conditions were for civic change to occur. Indeed, projects such as the AdvantAge Initiative constitute one important strategy for learning about change and how it occurs—through comparing and contrasting "best practices" to identify common conditions for success. Unfortunately, change is not only messy but there may very well be multiple pathways to reach common goals. Prescribing "one way" to achieve change would not only be inappropriate but deprive citizens of the opportunity to learn about and manage change on their own terms. The diversity of programs developed through the AdvantAge Initiative makes the task of comparison, in current parlance, rather dicey. During the initial period of the AdvantAge Initiative, 2000–2004, our research team had the opportunity to conduct additional case study research with a large number of aging programs throughout the United States and outside of the AI community network (Feldman et al. 2003). The goal of this research was to discover the elements of positive community change as exemplified in "best practice" projects. We defined the term "best practices," to mean exemplary initiative or practices, the study of which offers insight into how communities

- identify and understand
- raise awareness about
- organize and collaborate
- find the resources

to address the needs of a current and future aging population.

With respect to the process of program development, we observed programs initiated from the grass roots by a handful of dedicated pioneers, as contrasted with programs initiated "top down," with resources poured into a local community from above. With respect to approach, we observed programs ranging from planning only to service, to advocacy, to community development. With respect to issues, we observed programs focusing on transportation, home care, security, education, and long-term care, certainly a diverse sampling of the many kinds of programs that abound in communities around the United States.

While listing lessons learned and challenges faced in each community provides useful information for the reader, identifying common factors of success across the communities achieves the broader goal of synthesis and generalized learning we seek. With caution, therefore, I offer some general conclusions about the character of these successful change efforts. Not every program evinces every characteristic, which reinforces the assertion that we do not understand which factors are necessary, which are sufficient. Nevertheless, we have observed generally

- that these best practice programs have been initiated by leaders with situated knowledge of the environment for change
- that the right people in the right relationships are at the heart of change
- that the early leaders link this knowledge and these relationships through effective framing or marketing of issues
- that these relationships are sustained through effective communication and the creation of learning communities
- that community needs are met through the correct alignment of creatively defined resources with appropriately scaled solutions

SITUATED KNOWLEDGE

Some might simply call it savvy, others practical wisdom. Here, I refer to "situated knowledge" as the realization that beliefs, motivations, and actions are embedded in human interest. Some of the early so-called charismatic leaders of the projects reviewed were successful not because of some personality trait so much as a kind of cultural competence that enabled them to identify and reach out to include the "right" people. The right people were not merely the standard movers and shakers, though they were important to include. The right people were seen to include all those who might be affected by change, whether powerful or not—stakeholders, in the current language of community development.

Though a standard of inclusiveness was characteristic of the leaders, a practical acknowledgement of situated interests and political realities was also obvious. For the leaders of these projects, this competence was reflected in a willingness to employ whatever networks worked, "old boy" or whatever, to bring people aboard. Being able to identify and utilize mutual, overlapping self-interests to define common ground was a trait we observed among project leaders.

Moreover, this skill goes beyond simply knowing the right people or knowing the people who know the right people. It implies an ability to know the context and the constraints affecting the people one is asking to help. Project leaders made it easy for people to be involved and contribute.

While knowing the stakeholders and their interests was acknowledged by project leaders as an important element of success, it was also reported to be an ongoing challenge—one not simply solved at the beginning. It was noted that interests change, players change, and alliances are fluid. Hence, ongoing attention to the question "Is everybody here who needs to be?" was built into the process.

FRAMING ISSUES TO BUILD RELATIONSHIPS

Situated knowledge alone may not be enough to spur action. Simply knowing who to involve does not "get them there." Hence we observed that project leaders transformed this knowledge into action, by cultivating relationships, actively employing conveners with influence, using face-to-face communication and, last but not least, shirking timidity to ask for help. Project leaders noted the importance of knowing the audiences as a basis for articulating concepts correctly and felt that success would follow from enabling people to feel they are making a difference by getting involved. Looking for opportunities to collaborate, finding others to "pay your bills" was a common refrain offered by project leaders and participants.

SUSTAINING RELATIONSHIPS

Getting people involved was acknowledged as an important goal, while keeping them involved was acknowledged as perhaps the most difficult challenge. For the projects we observed, keeping people involved meant maintaining collaborative relationships with potential "competitors," mediating competing interests among those involved, and dealing with the loss of personnel due to the influences of outside forces.

A number of important elements served to sustain involvement over time in the projects we observed. Insightful leaders noted the importance of the mundane—make it social, make it fun—as well as the sublime—develop a culture of inclusiveness. Successful projects exhibited the character of the "learning community" and participants noted from the beginning that there would be no "right way"; that developing a program meant much more than simply adopting someone else's model. Rather than being an obstacle, conflict, when it occurred, was seen to provide a fertile ground for learning, an opportunity to try things in a different way.

A very important key to sustaining involvement was communication, and successful projects did an outstanding job in this area. Establishing an infrastructure for communication within and without was a priority, accomplished through minutes, memos, newsletters, telephone conversations, and effective use of the media.

ALIGNING RESOURCES AND SOLUTIONS

Moving from plans to action helps close the loop for those committed to change. Finding the resources to implement change, of course, took as much creativity as did other elements of the projects. Human or social capital was employed frequently as a resource for change, and savvy project participants found creative ways to solve problems without money. Indeed, project leaders cautioned against the assumption that public funding will always be available and worked carefully to mediate expectations of those desiring quick or massive change.

Of course, sustaining funding and support was reported as a major ongoing challenge to be faced. The key strategy used to sustain this support was, once again, centered on relationship building—reaching out for new partners, keeping older people involved, and expanding to reach underserved groups. While sustaining relationships and expanding to include others was an ongoing challenge reported by the projects, some projects were close to reaching the point of maturation and confronting, therefore, new dilemmas. For some the question was whether to leave a growth phase and enter an operational, management phase. For others, the question centered around the issue of professionalization—whether to diminish the role of volunteers in favor of paid staff or, better said, how to create the best fit between volunteer vs. professionally provided services for the clientele.

We have come full circle. We observed projects that started out as a glimmer of creativity and now are coping with the reality of their own institutionalization in the community. It seems important to note that many of the factors that I believe account for success are part and parcel of each phase of development and, in the end, simple and easy to summarize, at the risk of banality: acknowledge human interests, constantly work on building relationships, maintain an ethic of openness and inclusion, and find the correct alignment of resources and solutions. While these strategies are not guarantees of success, to be sure, they are certainly characteristic of the many outstanding projects that emerged from the AdvantAge Initiative and other community-based aging initiatives throughout the country.

᷈ A VERSION OF HOME ᷈

Folklorist Henry Glassie came upon a fine southern lady a few years ago
while he was engaged in a search for the meanings of home:

> I was once down in southern Kentucky, driving around and
> looking, as I did in those days, for old houses. I came to one
> and I wanted to take its picture. The woman of the house
> understood that I wished to take a picture of her home and so
> she assembled for me a little still life. Her name was Mae
> Young and in her still life what she did was to gather every-
> thing about her home that mattered. Boards didn't matter.
> The walls didn't matter. The fact that it conformed to one of
> Fred Kniffen's architectural types surely didn't matter to Mae
> Young. What mattered to her was her grandfather's little
> stoneware bottle. What mattered to her were the clumsily
> carved things that her grandfather gave her when she was a
> little girl. What mattered to her was the ring her grandfather
> beat out of pennies when he was a prisoner, starving in a
> Yankee prison. What mattered to her was a picture of an uncle
> whose name she didn't even remember. What mattered to her
> were the scissors she'd found when she was digging in the
> garden. What mattered to her was the family Bible. Wherever
> she is and those things are, that's home. Home doesn't need
> any walls at all. It can be a collection of possessions. (1995, 16)

CHAPTER 4

Participation: The Key to Community Building

Many attempts to create communities for older people rely solely on the so-called wisdom of expert consultants. Clearly, such efforts risk defeat for they fail to effectively incorporate the perspectives and voices of older adults who will be affected by the changes.

Yet, listening only to older voices entails certain risks as well. A community designed with and for seniors in 1975 will likely not meet the needs of aging Baby Boomers. Moreover, it is perhaps inherently undemocratic to create community institutions serving any particular age without considering the perspectives and wisdom of all ages, including children. Participation, in other words, is the key to effective community building.

Though opposing forces are at work, citizen participation is indeed growing throughout the world as grass roots activists demand more involvement in decisions that affect their lives. The word is still out, of course, as to whether civil society groups can tip the balance against nondemocratic interests vested in political power, capital, and sectarian ideologies.

One of the best definitions of participation clearly grounds the approach in a place-based framework:

> Participation ... provides a collaborative process by which community inhabitants reach common goals, engage in collective decisions, and create places, and these places, in turn, serve as material expressions of their collective efforts. (Feldman and Westphal, 2000)

There are multiple, compelling reasons why community development activists should promote the practice of citizen participation:

- Citizen participation helps frame issues in human terms.
- Citizen participation broadens accountability.
- Participation helps citizens learn the democratic process and how they fit in.
- Participation goes beyond the token form of "public input."
- Participation taps diverse modes of learning, interpretation, and creative solutions.
- Participation helps citizens ascend to an equal plane with holders of power.
- Participation helps build "democracy with a small d."

Whether a group is planning an elder-friendly community, a kid-friendly community, or simply a community for all ages, there are multiple tools available to engage citizens to participate in the process. These tools can, in fact, be utilized for a range of purposes:

- For conducting qualitative research into the daily experiences of specific target groups (the elderly, kids at risk, homeless persons, new citizens, etc.)
- For understanding the impact of programs and services on the daily lives of those for whom such services are intended
- For discovering and revealing to a wider audience the needs, skills, talents, and assets of individuals and groups who might otherwise be invisible to the mainstream public and persons in power
- For gathering and organizing diverse individuals and groups into processes designed to create a shared vision of a better future
- For simply helping a community learn about itself

Figure 4-1 illustrates a potpourri of citizen participation methods and techniques that can be put to some of the purposes in the preceding list. The range of participation methods is enormous and growing constantly through the creative efforts of community development activists worldwide.

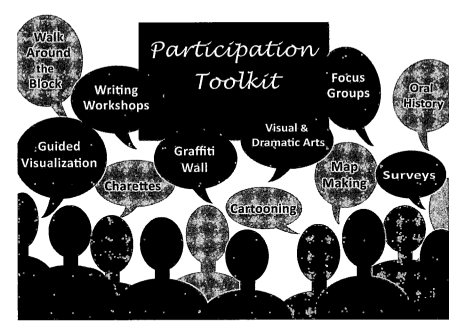

Figure 4-1 A Potpourri of Participation Methods

The drawing illustrates just a few of many exciting participation techniques that citizens can use to learn about their communities. A number of these approaches have been "incubated" in Bloomington, Indiana, and in other AdvantAge Initiative communities throughout the United States. While they have been used in planning processes oriented around the idea of elder-friendly communities, they can be applied to any issue of concern. Citizen-led map-making projects, for example, are often used by environmental activists to build awareness of changes in the natural environment (Flavelle 2002; cf. Maps with Teeth 1997). Focus groups are ubiquitous, of course, and can be applied to almost any particular issue of interest (Morgan and Krueger 1998). Oral history projects are proliferating worldwide and can help build a People's History that testifies to the value of ordinary lives or records events that risk erasure in official histories authored by groups in power (Slim and Thompson 1995).

If used well, the tools can also help individuals and groups build their own capacity. Meta learning will occur as participants learn about an issue through the tools and also learn about learning at the same time. In this sense, participation tools contribute to the development of learning communities.

SELECTING AND CRAFTING THE RIGHT TOOL FOR THE JOB

Facilitators and planning groups need to pay attention to the practical side of participation tools:

- Some tools work especially well with small groups but become hopelessly complex when applied to large groups.
- Some tools require real-time, simultaneous participation by all of the participants; others can serve a "drive-through" audience.
- Some tools are labor intensive to develop; others are ready-made.

Since there are multiple factors to consider when selecting and adapting a tool for a particular purpose, a checklist of questions is offered to help lead a practitioner to the most appropriate tool. Following the precautions of the old adage "give a kid a hammer and everything becomes a nail," the prospective facilitator or planner is encouraged to select and adapt tools in a deliberative fashion and not hammer everything in sight with one tool.

Criteria for Selecting Participation Tools

What is your desired outcome?

A. A vision for the future?

B. An understanding of the past?

C. An understanding of people's experiences?

D. An understanding of people's preferences?

E. An understanding of the impact of a service, program, or change in policy?

F. Identification of a broad range of issues?

G. ... or a deeper understanding of specifics?

H. An advocacy position?

I. A proposal for funding?

What kind of product do you need?

A. A scientifically valid report?
B. A performance?
C. A media product?
D. A white paper?
E. A public exhibition or event?
F. A proposal?

How much time do you have?

A. How much time do you have to prepare for the task?
B. How much time are you asking for from the participants?

What will it cost?

A. Will you use experts or paid facilitators?
B. Will there be facilities costs?
C. Will there be supply costs?
D. Will there be food costs?

How diverse is the group of participants you hope to attract?

A. By cultural background?
B. By age?
C. By education and literacy?
D. By race?
E. By tenure in the community?
F. By income?
G. By political persuasion?
H. By degree of power and influence?
I. By ability?

How many participants do you want to include?

    A. High numbers across a diverse range?

    B. A small, but representative, sample?

    C. A random sample?

What kind of engagement will be expected of participants?

    A. Will they be required to talk in front of others?

    B. Might they feel intimidated in certain situations or settings?

    C. What are the risks of participation?

    D. How much disclosure is required of participants?

    E. Is participation egalitarian?

    F. Will it be "one and done" or "multiple phases?"

    G. How much fun will people have doing this?

Walking through these questions with a planning group will begin to help narrow down the choices. In following sections are provided some examples of tools that vary in purpose, cost, diversity of participants, and mode of participation. These tools have been used in actual elder-friendly community projects but can be adapted, and *should* be adapted, to meet local needs and circumstances.

TOOLS FOR VISIONING

Many community development projects start with a vision. Too often, however, that vision is the brainchild of a single, albeit sometimes powerful or charismatic leader. Carrying out such a vision for a community can be a good thing. But getting everyone on board to claim that vision as their own can be a challenge. In worst-case scenarios even the best ideas can be sabotaged by those who were never asked to share in the process of creating them.

For at least a decade, "visioning" has been a hot topic and, I daresay, most every reader has participated in a visioning exercise sometime during his/her recent career. Airport bookshop shelves have long been filled with the latest and presumably greatest guides to "visionary management." So what more can be said about the practice of visioning? Perhaps not much, except to point out that a critical distinction between corporate visioning and community visioning tends to get lost. A crucial question lies at the center of community visioning processes: *Whose vision?*

Corporate planners do sometimes speak to the importance of creating a *shared* vision to spur enthusiasm and enable productive collective action (teamwork). Many visioning tools have been developed for use in such strategic planning processes. And, along with the value of engaging employees and shareholders in this process, progressive companies sometimes include reference to social values as being on a par with sales. Yet, in the end, corporate visioning is essentially an internal process; the public is not fully empowered to participate, and someone at the top gets to decide whose vision will be carried forward.

Community visioning, on the other hand, should be seen as a *civic* process, with citizen participation at the core. While it would be naïve to suggest that power and influence do not enter into the selection of a vision, the goal of citizen participation is to work toward a vesting of that power not in individuals but in the process itself and its elements: the power of imagination, the power of discourse, the power of collective action, the power of both specialized and ordinary knowledge and experience.

Seeing community visioning as one component, then, of a broader process of democratic (small "d") community development is our starting point. Answering the question "Whose vision?" is job one (to steal another corporate metaphor). Creating the vision is job two. Moving the vision to action is job three.

If we fail to include the widest possible circle of voices in the beginning, we risk, at the best, alienating those for whom the vision is supposed to apply and, at the worst, a sabotage of the vision by those angered by the neglect of their views. If we fail to move the vision forward to action, we have simply engaged in a meaningless, albeit stimulating exercise in science fiction.

In short, we need to place visioning within the broader context of a comprehensive community development model that moves from:

VOICE   to   VISION   to   ACTION

VISIONING IS NOT JUST ABOUT THE FUTURE

There is another popular section in your standard airport bookshop—the one labeled "futurists." We all enjoy reading about what the future holds and get excited about the many wonders ahead. Yet, what is too often ignored by futurists is the notion that our future is necessarily tied to our present and, by extension, our past. Metaphorically, the future is pictured as somehow coming toward us, rather than the other way around. We are exhorted to be prepared and, thusly, disfranchised, since that future is, somehow, not of our own doing.

This is to say that visioning needs to be embedded in real time. There are, indeed, several reasons why we need to pay attention to visioning as merely part of the unfolding of time and events:

- A vision needs to be realistic. This may sound contradictory, but for citizens to take the process seriously, it needs to connect with real life experience and knowledge. Regretfully, there is much cynicism out there, especially among marginalized citizens and neighborhoods (people in poverty, vulnerable elders, and others). These groups have been on the receiving end of other people's unrealized visions for a long time and, legitimately, will enter into new visioning with suspicion and caution.
- A useful vision must acknowledge the past and connect with the present. Even though the "good old days" might not have been so good at the time, it is essential to acknowledge the historical experiences of the people whom you invite to help create a vision for the future. This serves several purposes:
  - o It models an essential community value by honoring our elders.
  - o It informs us about all those previous visions that never came to pass.
  - o Or, pleasantly, it informs us about how what we have today may indeed be the product of someone's earlier vision.
  - o It dampens the negative effect of sidebar cynics who can sabotage the effort through "we tried that before" thinking.
  - o It helps create a learning community in which everyone has access to all knowledge.

VISION IS RELATED TO THAT OTHER OVERUSED "V" WORD: VALUES

While it may seem obvious, it is important to note that creating a vision for the future is an exercise in the expression of values. For citizens who have not been involved in such processes, we should not assume too much. Some people might interpret a visioning exercise as some kind of workshop that has people *predicting*, not selecting, the future. Asking someone to see into the future does not guarantee they will see a "desired" future, but rather a bleak one. Moreover, different cultural groups will attach a variety of meanings to this idea of visioning. Think about the Native American vision quest, for example, and what that might connote. It certainly does not suggest a collective process, but an individual one, though subject to "expert" interpretation by elders.

Hence, it needs to be made clear to participants that what they are being invited to do is to simply express themselves about "the way it was," "the way it is," and the "way things should be." Fancy buzzwords are not always necessary.

Since we are seeking citizens' opinions about a desired future, we are asking people to place a value on something. Different visions suggest differing values, of course, and so the process helps clarify and reveal a range of individual and community values. As such, this kind of exercise begins to hit close to home and, hence, an environment of tolerance for diverse values is critical to the success of the venture. In many ways we are not just one, big, happy family, and it is useful to think through the implications of this for community visioning. Take the issue of nursing homes, for example: *Many people feel that nursing homes are an abomination and that we should imagine a future in which they do not exist.*

On the other hand: *A future without nursing homes might be a pretty scary vision for the sandwich generation daughter who is single handedly raising teenage children and caring for a parent with dementia.*

Clearly, nurturing a trusting environment that will accommodate an airing of all values, dearly held, will be important to the facilitator.

How people present their opinions in public is another aspect of this values dimension, where cultural factors may also come in to play. The way you present the task of visioning is important. Are you asking people to express their personal desires; imagine *themselves* as old? Or are you asking people to speak for others who may be old? It makes a difference in the product you achieve:

- Some people do not feel entitled to speak for themselves, and may have never been asked.
- Some people feel that it is selfish or brash to express what they need over what they might feel are the needs of others.
- Some people do not feel qualified to speak for others.

- Some people feel qualified to speak for others, in fact *only* speak for others, and, in fact, may not actually be qualified!

If there is a rule of thumb, it is that "it takes all kinds" and a diverse visioning process will tap into all of these perspectives. Indeed, rather than prescribing a particular approach, the practitioner should simply acknowledge publicly that citizens assume different styles, model respect for these different styles, and interpret the information received within the appropriate context from which it emerged. All of these human expressions are authentic in their own right.

Despite the authenticity of the expressions, you can do a service by pointing out this dilemma and asking people to try on all the hats if they can; speak for oneself *as* an old person (or future one) *and* speak for others whom you may know or think you know. The issue provides a "learning moment" in which you can discuss the classic individual/community dichotomy and the role that cultural differences play in public settings.

Another way around this dilemma is to provide a range of alternative modes of participation. *One big workshop* is not necessarily the best approach for it will likely exclude certain citizens from participation. If time and resources allow, promote multiple modes of expression and plan for a mechanism to bring them all together in a common document. In following sections are provided some specific tools that communities can use to create a vision for a livable, lifespan community. Beyond creating a future vision, other tools provided can help a neighborhood or community to learn about its own past and about present conditions, all essential steps to a community-building process.

TOOL: GUIDED VISUALIZATION

Summary: Guided imagery is a low cost method that a single facilitator can use with small to large groups. The exercise can be completed in as few as 15 minutes, though it should always be followed by discussion and interpretation. The process invites listeners to relax, close their eyes, and travel through the mind's eye with a "guide" for a brief period of time. In this exercise participants travel through what they might imagine to be an "elder-friendly community." It requires a quiet room and a willing audience. While a paid facilitator is not required, a group leader with experience is helpful. The guided imagery "script" should be printed out beforehand so that it can be practiced and read to the group.

While typically thought of as a therapeutic tool, useful in promoting relaxation, healing, and stress reduction, guided visualization has found wide use as a visioning tool for strategic planning. Briefly, guided visualization or imagery takes participants through a "mental map" of unrealized dreams. Participants temporarily disengage from the outside world and attempt to visualize a new community through the mind's eye. The script provides key questions along the way as participants silently imagine this new terrain.

By way of introduction, the facilitator should describe what the exercise will involve. Participants should be invited to move their chairs apart, place both feet on the floor, hands resting comfortably on laps. "Let your head bobble for a few seconds then find a comfortable resting position on your shoulders. Now close your eyes and begin to enter into your own zone of peace and quiet."

In the following script, authored by friend and colleague Jane Clay, participants gather for a bus tour of their community of the future.

Visioning an Elder-friendly Community

Jane Clay

Evergreen Institute on Elder Environments

Visions of our preferred future are the pictures we carry in our minds and hearts of how we want something to be when we have gotten it right. Our visions inspire us to work toward the ideal. So now, we are going to picture a preferred future in which people are valued and their needs are met throughout their lifespan. Then we'll share the dreams so we can get to work on making it happen.

Please settle comfortably in your chair. Leave pencils and papers on the table, hands in your lap. Now close your eyes ... relax ... listen ... and imagine what our community will look like when we get it right.

(Start Music—"Quiet City" by Aaron Copland)

It is the future—the year 2010. A very special tour arrives in our community. Filling the bus are leaders from across the state, the country, and the world. They are here to see our community, the best community for people of all ages in which to grow up, live and work, and grow old.

The bus pulls up to the curb and stops so someone can get on. This someone is the tour guide who will be showing the guests around. The tour guide is . . . YOU! And why not you? You are responsible for the progress this community has made. You were an integral member of the team that pulled everyone together, dreamed big dreams, that got people excited and eager to use their gifts and talents to build a community that's a good place to live and grow old. Now these leaders, from all over, have asked you to show them what your community is like and how it was done. You're happy to be pointing out all the ways your community provides a good quality of life for everyone, young and old. And at each stop you explain how your group has influenced the community's progress in this area.

You see people of all ages. They are:
Going to work . . . Where do they work? What kind of work do they do? How do they get there?
What are these workplaces like? How do people work together on the job? How are young and old working together to make the work they do more effective?
(How did your group improve workplaces for all in your community?)

Children going to school . . . What do the schools look like? What activities are going on? What are the children learning? Who are they learning from? How are the students, teachers, parents, neighbors and administrators interacting? How is the role of educating youth viewed by those who are not parents?
(How did your group improve schools in your community?)

Seniors . . . Where do they live? What are they doing? How are they getting around and finding services? With whom are they interacting? What quality of life do they enjoy? How are they viewed by the rest of the community?
(How did your group improve life for elders in your community?)

Teenagers . . . What are they busy doing? How are they spending their time and energy? What do they value about their community? For what are they valued by the community? How do they interact with those older and younger than they are?

(How did your group touch the lives of teenagers in your community?)

People in neighborhoods . . . What do the neighborhoods look like? The streets? The houses? How do people feel about their neighborhoods? Do they feel safe? Are they proud to live there? What are the people doing together?
(How did your group improve the neighborhoods in your community?)

People are going places to enjoy leisure time . . . Where are they going? What are they doing? How do they interact with others? What kinds of opportunities for leisure do they have? In the arts? Recreation? Outdoors? In all seasons? How are people getting there?
(How did your group impact the opportunities for leisure enjoyment in your community?)

People are volunteering . . . helping each other. Why are they doing this? What are they doing for each other and with each other? Who are the recipients of these efforts?
(How did your group improve the ways people help each other in your community?)

Important decisions are being made in your community . . . What are the decisions being made about? Who's involved in the decisions? What processes are being used? Do people like the results, process, and the way they are treated?
(How did your group improve the way community decisions are made?)

People are worshipping . . . What impact does faith have on the life of the community? How have differences in faiths been resolved?
(How did your group impact the role of faith in your community?)

The people you see are, as always, a mix of races, philosophies, ages and perspectives. How do different people and groups of people show they appreciate, understand, and value others?
(How did your group help your community identify and appreciate its diversity and deal with problems in this area?)

People are coming and going at civic meeting centers around town . . . city hall, the courthouse, libraries, arts center . . . What's going on there? Who's participating?
(How did your group improve opportunities for participation?)

People are going to places of health care . . . What is their state of health? What do they do to promote their health and wellness? Where is health care provided? Who receives health care? How are health decisions being made?

(How did your group solve problems about health care for all and promote the well-being of the whole community?)

What is the status of the environment? Who speaks for the environment? How have the decisions made about the environment affected the quality of life in the community?
(How did your group impact the decisions made about the environment?)

The tour's almost over . . . You've covered it all . . . or nearly all. As the bus heads back to your departure place, you swing by one more spot. You don't want the visitors to miss this . . . it's the part of the community of which you're most proud . . . What do you show them and what do you tell them?

Now the tour is over. It's time for you to leave the bus. Before getting off, you walk down the aisle for personal good-byes. One by one the visitors thank you. One by one, they tell you how they liked what they saw. "Congratulations," they say. "You got it right! This is what we want, too. We want communities that work just as well for all members as yours does!"
                                        —END—

When participants are brought back to "reality," the fruits of this exercise are harvested through group discussion and debriefing. Participants may wish to take a brief break at this point, but they are reminded to keep the images from the tour in their minds, in preparation for sharing them with others.

Depending upon your goals and the size of the group, the following exercises can be done with the participants.

Host an overall discussion with the entire group, asking people to share key elements of their dreams—things they saw that made them feel good about the community (10–15 minutes).

- Then ask participants whether they feel optimistic that some of these elements and dreams can be realized in this community.
- What are the barriers?
- What would it take to change?
- How would you create this future?

Or, break a larger group into small groups of five to eight (at tables) to conduct a poster project (30–45 minutes plus 15–45 minutes for "reporting out").

- Distribute one sheet of newsprint and multiple colored markers to each table.
- Ask the group to spend the first 10 minutes sharing the things they saw on tour.
- Make sure each table selects a recorder to take notes from this discussion, listing key words they hear as people share their "maps."

After 10 minutes, ask each group to now plan and execute a drawing or map that describes what they feel would be a "good place to grow old." Explain that they will have to determine what scale is important first of all: Will they try to draw an entire city or town? A neighborhood? A single facility? Anything is acceptable, of course, since we seek principles that can be applied in any environment, small to large.

Monitor the groups to make sure they do not linger too long in planning. Some groups will forge right ahead, others will choose to carefully plan and only draw toward the end. After 20–30 minutes, the groups should be near completion. A short break is sometimes desired here.

In round robin fashion, allow two people from each group to stand and display their maps for the entire audience. The speakers should narrate what the maps say or mean and answer questions that audience members may pose (5 minutes per group).

Following this exhibition period, the facilitator will then lead an overall discussion to summarize key points, things learned through the exercise. Using newsprint to record these points, for later use of course, the facilitator might say: *"Ok, let's list the key elements of a lifespan (or elder-friendly, or kid-friendly, etc.) community."* Some examples that might emerge:

- old people are everywhere (see Alexander, Ishikawa, and Silverstein 1977)
- universal accessibility
- people can get to stores, services, cultural and recreational facilities
- old people are respected in interactions with others
- kids and old people interact frequently
- people can die at home or in their residence of choice

- the environment promotes physical exercise
- locally grown and healthy foods are eaten

These key elements, retained for later use, can provide an excellent starting point for subsequent strategic planning efforts. If the workshops continue throughout the day or are set up as a series, the facilitator can help participants explore these ideas further, according to interests and energies of the group.

- This can be a link to a discussion of surveying the community to see whether these principles are, in fact, being followed (some good guides are available).
- If the project is linked to the AdvantAge Initiative survey process, it can provide a basis for identifying key issues around which particular survey questions can be utilized.
- Small task groups can begin to take similar issues and explore them in greater depth to identify key stakeholders, barriers, helping forces, and potential action steps—reporting back to the large group at a designated point in time.
- The posters can be matted and displayed in a public venue that may serve to continue and expand the community dialogue.

TOOL: THE GRAFFITI WALL

Summary: This tool can be multipurpose. It involves the placement of a blank mural in a public venue with a simple set of instructions and available colored markers. It is inexpensive and can serve as a "drive-through" alternative to a workshop or collective meeting. It provides a compelling visual product and enables participation by people who otherwise might not be involved: nonliterate, kids, workers with busy schedules, diverse cultures, etc.

This technique provides a fun and engaging way for citizens to express themselves about an issue or create a vision for a desired future. Of course, the "data" retrieved are not a random sample, particularly if it is gathered in a more private space such as a senior center, school, workplace, etc.

The issue about which information is sought is clarified through the placement of a question in large, bold print at the top of the mural. In a project in Bloomington, Indiana, the question posed, as reflected in the image above, was the following:

Figure 4-2   Graffiti Wall

What makes a neighborhood healthy?

Using newsprint (which can be sometimes obtained free from the local newspaper office—ask for the ends of the rolls), post the blank paper wall at a level that can be accessed by people of all heights and abilities, including kids and users of wheelchairs. The Bloomington mural measured approximately 5 feet by 14 feet. Seek a smooth wall, and use masking tape around the entire edge to prevent fraying. Make a test mark on the paper to make sure the ink does not bleed through.

Attach markers on strings to various points along the wall or place markers for use on a nearby ledge or shelf. If needed, place a laminated instructional placard nearby for curious people who want to know more about why this is being done before committing to express themselves.

In the Bloomington project, the mural was posted in conjunction with a multimedia display on aging at the local community arts center. The mural was placed in a hallway utilized by the public attendees over the course of two weeks. Other venues, depending on your target audience, might include:

- Public malls
- Senior centers/community centers
- Schools
- Lobbies in municipal buildings, city hall, etc.
- Public transportation lobbies
- Work place cafeterias
- Outdoor spaces, kiosks, etc.
- Store windows along heavily traveled sidewalks
- Hospital/medical center lobbies

Some other questions that might be placed on the mural for a response could be the following:

— What is your favorite place in this community?
— What would make _____ town more elder-friendly?
— What would make _____ town a good place for all ages?
— What do you like best about this senior center?

Ask provocative questions that anyone can answer and provide an opportunity for pictorial responses as well. Make sure the mural is monitored regularly to prevent vandalism, weather damage, marker theft, etc. This may influence the choice of a location.

When it is determined that sufficient time has been provided for responses (or when the wall is filled with responses), the mural is removed and the responses transcribed to an alternate format. While the method is not scientific, of course, one can count similar responses and report them by frequency or use this to identify key themes. Pictures of graphic elements from the mural can be taken and scanned into reports. The report might be a section in a larger community planning document, a brief pamphlet, even a Web site or a newspaper insert. The more visually appealing the document, the more likely it is to be read by the public. That is one reason why graffiti walls are a great way to raise public awareness and interest.

TOOL: COLLAGES

(With appreciation to Mia Oberlink, Center for Home Care Policy and Research.)

Asking individuals to create a personal collage on a particular subject is an excellent way to provide an alternative mode of expression, particularly for people who might be intimidated by other opportunities for public expression. Collages can give voice to participants' views of what attributes make a community a good place in which to grow older. Invite participants to create a collage representing their view of an "elder-friendly community," and then use the results for a group discussion. Participants can incorporate photographs, images from magazines, newspaper clippings, hand-drawn pictures, and other materials to express their views. Each collage serves as a means to understand an individual's perspective, as well as to highlight themes that are meaningful to groups of participants. The collages provide an excellent foil for opening up a community conversation about these significant issues. The gender, city, and age-grouping of each originator is provided.

The national AdvantAge Initiative began with a series of national focus groups conducted in four diverse U.S. communities. Three age-stratified groups and a fourth group of community leaders were constituted in each city. Prospective participants were invited to create and bring a collage on the subject of "an elder-friendly community." The outstanding response to the request generated a diverse collection of images and stimulated interesting discussion in each group. Some collages emphasized recreation and leisure (actually a minority). Several emphasized community services and infrastructure. Some emphasized spiritual themes. Many emphasized social and familial connections. The collages and the more specific data from the national focus groups resulted in the identification of four "domains" of an elder-friendly community that, to this day, provides a framework for community research and planning efforts throughout the United States, as discussed in Chapter 3.

As with the graffiti wall products, collages lend themselves very well to further use in crafting and stimulating community conversations about aging and other issues. They can become Web-based products, laminated for public exhibits, reproduced for print publications, or even printed as place mats and used to stimulate conversation around a dinner table!

TOOL: MAPMAKING AND THE WALKABOUT—AN INTERGENERATIONAL EXPLORATION OF COMMUNITY

Mapmaking and maps seem to have a wide appeal across the generations. Perhaps it is our fascination with our personal place in the universe—"this is my home"—that motivates this interest. Perhaps it is the visual, nonlinear nature of maps that draws upon our right-brain, creative side, and connects with bodily experience. Whatever the reason, maps and mapmaking can provide fertile material for discussions of community life and neighborhood improvement. As Doug Abberley notes (*Maps with Teeth* 1997), maps can exert a compelling power to influence public discussion and, too often, we have turned over the power to create maps to the experts. Abberley's goal is to place this power back into the hands of those who are affected by change. He wants to create "maps with teeth." A brief overview of an intergenerational mapmaking project in a Bloomington Public Housing neighborhood follows. The goal of the project was to engage children in an exploration and critical examination of their neighborhood as a basis for finding out what they believe can be done to improve it.

Crestmont Discovery Project: Bloomington, Indiana, 2004

Goals:

- Assist young members of the Crestmont Boys and Girls Club to explore and learn about the physical, natural, and social environment of the club and the surrounding neighborhood.
- Connect Boys and Girls Club members with neighborhood elders.

- Empower youth to identify and act upon their ideas for neighborhood improvement.

Activities:

Day One—Mapping your Neighborhood

Day Two—A Walk around the Block: Neighborhood Exploration and Documentation

Day Three—Debriefing and Social Action Discussion

Resources Needed:

- Responsible chaperones for the "walk around the block" phase
- Volunteers or older students to assist with preparation of materials and group process
- Neighborhood GIS map(s)
- Disposable cameras
- Prepared neighborhood checklist booklet
- Digital camera or video camera (optional)
- Art supplies: newsprint, markers, colored pencils, mat paper
- Community volunteers on the receiving end of visitations

Preparation:

Going into somebody else's neighborhood "to help them" is risky business, however sincere one's motivation. Hence, building a linkage with an authentic neighborhood institution is the critical first step in a project like this. It might be a church or synagogue. It might be a community-based organization. Whatever the partner might be, its legitimacy within the eyes of the neighborhood residents is important to success. Government institutions might appear to be good partners from the outside but actually be the objects of suspicion from within.

In Bloomington, this project was organized around an Indiana University service-learning *Field Seminar in Cultural Documentation*, offered by the author and his colleague Dr. Inta Carpenter, of the Indiana University Folklore Institute. Crestmont is a public housing community that has been subject to stigmatizing attitudes within the larger community over its 25-year history. The approach to the community was taken through the Resident Council, authorized by the Housing Authority as the official voice of the neighborhood. Through the council, we were directed to the Crestmont Boys and Girls Club, a satellite of the larger, downtown club, and housed in a converted duplex/townhome within the public housing stock of homes and apartments. The director of the Boys and Girls Club was thrilled with the idea of the project and offered staff assistance with gaining access to and support of the children.

Approximately one month prior to the event, the instructors and students secured a GIS (Geographic Information System) map of the target neighborhood from the City of Bloomington Utilities Department. The map was intentionally plotted to include the fringe areas beyond the public housing community itself, in order to explore and challenge the children's notions of their neighborhood boundaries. Data plotted onto the GIS map included streets, street names, house footprints and numbers, railroads, and other structures/features of significance. Utilities and other layers of data are not needed for this project.

The first step is to secure a roll of newsprint (obtain "ends" from your local newspaper office) and, with masking tape, erect a paper wall approximately 8–10 feet by 4 feet. This mural will remain in place for the time needed to transfer the GIS map to the blank paper wall.

The standard GIS map (approximately 24 inches by 36 inches) needs to be cut into sections that are sized 8-1/2 inches by 11 inches in order to create transparencies that can next be projected onto the large blank mural. Using colored markers, the field seminar students created a giant map of the neighborhood on the blank mural. Different colors were used for streets, house footprints, and other structures of significance (swimming pools, parks, etc.). Each house included its corresponding house number. This project requires several person/hours of labor but is very enjoyable for the students. (The college students were introduced to the neighborhood in prior "walk-throughs" and were required to write about their impressions in student journals and through haiku.)

In addition to the "big map," we prepared and duplicated for each prospective youth participant a checklist to be employed on a chaperoned exploratory walk through the neighborhood. The booklet provided each child with a set of questions to be answered as they walk through the neighborhood, not unlike a scavenger hunt. In the spring of 2004, the theme for the project was "Alice's Adventure through Wonderland."

Day One: Initial Mapmaking Exercise

Following the creation of a flyer/permission slip to be sent home with the children, the Boys and Girls Club staff helped recruit and gather children for Day One of the exercise (done as an after-school project). For this project, we displayed the giant map at the club on two adjoining tables, as wall space was insufficient for posting it. Before breaking into smaller groups, we facilitated a general discussion in front of the map with the children. Then we asked our college students to work with small groups of kids, each child being provided with markers, colored pencils, and a blank sheet of drawing paper (18 inches by 24 inches). The following script was provided to small group leaders.

After you get the kids' attention, and before passing out materials, you can start with some trigger questions (trigger questions are just examples—try to use them to get beyond yes and no responses):

- Does everyone here live in this neighborhood? How many?
- Was anyone born in this neighborhood?
- If not, when did you move here?
- Who has lived here the longest?
- Find out who is the newest resident.
- How did you learn about your new neighborhood?
  — Explore with your bike?
  — Ask questions?
  — Find a friend?
- What's the best thing about this neighborhood?
- What would you change if you were in charge?
- So just what is this neighborhood?
  — What is its name?
  — Does anyone know other names for this place?
  — Does anyone know how it got these names?
  — What is your favorite name?
- What would you say are the boundaries of this neighborhood? Where does it end?

— Which direction is north?

— And so on for the other three boundaries?

Then say, "OK—now we're going to have you put your own map on paper so you can tell people about your neighborhood. Tomorrow, we're going on an adventure walk to see things first hand, but today, we're walking through the neighborhood with our imaginations."

Pass out the materials, ask them to wait for further directions. Say something like: "You have the entire piece of paper to work on. You have lots of different colors to work with. Before you start, close your eyes and picture your house or apartment. You can be a bird flying above it and looking down. Or you can imagine walking out the front door. Think about where your neighborhood begins and ends. It might be at a street or at a building. When you are ready, open your eyes and draw a map of your neighborhood. You can put anything you want in the map. There's plenty of time."

After a while, say, "When you think you are done ... put some notes on the map that show things that are important to you: your favorite place, your scariest place, where your best friend lives, where you spend a lot of time, those kinds of things." If time allows, ask the kids to share their maps with each other, discussing some of the questions asked previously.

When everyone is done, say: "Don't forget tomorrow we will be meeting at 4 pm for the walk. Don't be late since we have people waiting for us at different places to help us in the adventure."

After the children complete the exercise, drawing their own maps of the neighborhood, post the maps and/or pictures of the exercise around the club. We used a digital camera profusely to document the process for and with the kids.

An example of a neighborhood map, derived from another workshop, is shown in Figure 4-3.

Day Two: A Walk around the Block

In preparation for this exercise, the planning team discussed and decided upon a small number of destinations and themes to be explored

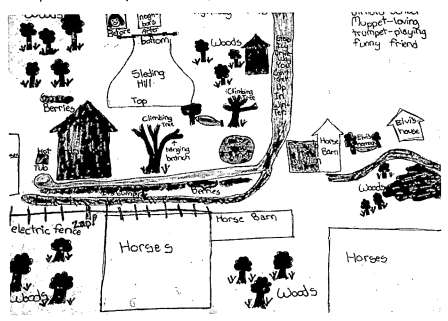

Figure 4-3 A Kid's View of the Neighborhood

by small student groups in a chaperoned walk around the block. In the 2004 exercise, the following challenges were identified:

- One group would identify water features in the neighborhood. (This involved prearranged meetings with city officials from utilities and parks/recreation to meet the students and help them learn about a water supply tower and a community swimming pool.)
- One group would visit a straw bale house being constructed in the neighborhood by Habitat for Humanity and visit to interview Mrs. Harris, one of the oldest residents of the neighborhood.
- One group would receive a "behind the scenes" tour of the Opportunity House thrift shop.
- One group would visit the community kitchen and also a one-stop grocery to do research on price comparisons retrieved ahead for other major groceries outside of the neighborhood.

Prior to beginning the discovery walks, each student was provided the booklet and offered an orientation to the questions asked and the kinds of observations expected of them during the walk. Gathered around the "giant map," we had a general discussion of neighborhood boundaries and key landmarks. The students were informed that, upon their return, they would be asked to transfer their observations to the giant map. A disposable flash camera was provided to each group. One group was accompanied by a staff person to serve as a videographer.

Following the organized chaos of gathering the kids and constituting the groups, the discovery walk was begun. A ratio of two adults to four children was maintained. Adults in each group were provided, in advance, with directions for their specific destination.

The groups returned to the Club after approximately 45 minutes. They took part in the normal snack routine at the Club, and those not returning home worked with the giant map, using markers and colored pencils to embellish the map, label destinations, and record observations. Several located and labeled their own homes on the map as well as the homes of their friends.

Day Three: Debriefing and Social Action

On Day Three of the project, the kids reconvened around the giant map and continued, initially, to add notations and labels. A general discussion was facilitated to draw reactions from the kids regarding things they learned about the neighborhood from their walk. Once again, they discussed favorite places, places that need to be cleaned up, places to play, places to shop, places to meet their friends, etc. With encouragement, solicited comments were transferred to the map.

In a final component of the discussion, the kids were asked to think carefully about four "big and cool" ideas for neighborhood improvement (Race and Torma 1998). The question "what would make this a good neighborhood to live in" generated four core responses:

- "More gardens like Mrs. Harris's."
    - o Mrs. Harris, the elder interviewed by one group, maintains a lush and attractive flower garden outside of her apartment.
- "The trash dumpster should be moved from the circle."
    - o Near the playground sits a large dumpster subject to use by people who have no connection with the neighborhood.
- "People should be nicer to each other."
- "More park benches for old people are needed."

Digital photos drawn from the previous two days, downloaded and matted for the students, were distributed and provided some immediate feedback and reinforcement of the enthusiasm for the project. The kids felt rewarded and acknowledged in a very direct way through this little gift.

Follow-up and Social Action

Two subsequent events at the main Boys and Girls Club provided an opportunity to showcase the work of the kids: the annual awards banquet and a career opportunity fair. The university students assembled project artifacts into a display to be erected and our videographer created a 15-minute video with titles that could be shown on a laptop.

Another public event in the neighborhood, a street fair/service fair, provided an opportunity to share the project results with a broader audience beyond Club kids and their parents. At this display, a voting table was set up highlighting the four big and cool ideas and residents voted, with beans, for their top choices.

At a subsequent meeting of the Residents Council for the public housing community, two of the project participants were assisted to give a presentation, with the video, on the project and reveal the results of the informal street fair poll. The kids' presentation was so well received they were asked to consider providing some leadership for the creation of a kids' council for the neighborhood.

When informed at a staff meeting about the problems associated with the dumpster, the housing authority director installed video surveillance and created a campaign for residents to track license plates of illegal dumpster users. Eventually, the dumpster was moved off the cul-de-sac.

Lastly, a local artist who specializes in public and collaborative art projects was engaged to work with the growing group of stakeholders to create public art with the children that would make the club "a more welcoming and familiar" environment. An additional two years of collaborative planning and design with the children and funding from multiple sources (city, National Endowment for the Arts, others) culminated in the erection of the "Bicycle Arch," a colorful and whimsical sculpture that now serves as an iconic entrance to the club and has brought positive recognition to the neighborhood.

Additional collaborative public arts projects are now in progress, including new features in a toddler park and a flock of magnetic birds

Figure 4-4 Debriefing the Walkabout

for the water tower that will symbolize the renaissance of the neighborhood and, it is hoped, recast the traditional stigmatized name of the community (Pigeon Hill) with a positive spin.

Multiple learning goals can be met through a project of this nature.
Young people are introduced to elders in the neighborhood and have
their own knowledge and experience affirmed and validated. They are
enabled to work with older students as well as adults in an egalitarian
way. Through their research, they identify both community problems
and community assets and, with follow-up, build trust with adults to help
them work through neighborhood problems.

Figure 4-5 Dedication of the Crestmont Bicycle Arch

TOOL: THE CHARRETTE

Bill Lennertz and Aarin Lutzenhizer, authors of *The Charrette Handbook* (2006), define the charrette and the origin of the term:

> The charrette is a multi-day planning process during which an interdisciplinary professional design team creates a complete and feasible plan that reflects the input of all interested parties by engaging them in a series of feedback loops. The term "charrette" is derived from a French word meaning "cart" and refers to the final intense work effort expended by art and architecture students to meet a project deadline. At the École des Beaux Arts in Paris during the 19th century, proctors circulated with carts to collect final drawings, and students would jump on the charrette with their work and frantically put finishing touches on their drawings. This intense burst of activity is similar to the atmosphere of the

modern charrette. Today's charrettes offer much more than just a quick fix. The result is lasting, transformative community change.

Perhaps the first use of the charrette to design an "elder-friendly" neighborhood was the Evergreen charrette held in Bloomington, Indiana, in 1997 and described in Stafford (2001). The charrette charged participants over several days to incorporate the "Evergreen design principles," derived from 18 months of community participation research, in an effort to remake a downtown neighborhood into an intergenerational environment.

In 2007, students and faculty of the School of Architecture, Southern Illinois University at Carbondale, assisted the Egyptian Area Agency on Aging and Carbondale residents in rethinking the built infrastructure of the community. Following the creation of asset inventories, students envisioned new retail businesses, sidewalks, housing types, and landscaping to make the community age-friendly.

In 2009, perhaps the most ambitious charrette initiative ever undertaken occurred in Atlanta, Georgia, through the auspices of the Area Agency on Aging, a unit of the Atlanta Regional Plan Commission (ARC), with the masterful coordination of consultants Kathryn Lawler and M. Scott Ball. As a recipient of funding from the Robert Wood Johnson Foundation, the Atlanta region had been engaged in three years of preliminary planning through the *Community Partnerships for Older Adults* initiative. Through the effective use of AdvantAge Initiative survey data and GIS mapping technologies, the Atlanta regional project engaged hundreds of citizens and multiple neighborhood groups in reconfiguring long-term care as a community-wide issue.

In 2008, Lawler began mobilizing interests, stakeholders, and funders to "re-imagine" Atlanta as a "lifelong community." With the support of the Atlanta Regional Commission and numerous funders, Lawler retained the services of one of the most prominent New Urbanist planning/design firms in the United States, DPZ (Duany Plater-Zyberk), to plan a multiday charrette process. Lawler then connected with several private developers who owned properties in the region and were interested in participating in a process that would assist them in envisioning the development potential, in collaboration with residents and in partnership with the prestigious design firm. The services of DPZ and the potential for reducing neighborhood opposition to development added value to the developers' projects and, as a consequence, they provided significant funding for the project.

Figure 4-6 André Duany at Atlanta Lifelong Communities Charrette, February 2009

Over a nine-day period in February 2009, nearly 1,000 Atlantans participated in a multiday, staged process to reimagine six specific neighborhoods as "lifelong communities." This would involve serious attention to the promotion of a wide range of housing and transportation/mobility options and the creation of environments that promote physical activity, social interaction, and easy access to health care. The charrette process was very carefully designed to provide an environment in which designers would be attuned to both citizen ideas and concerns, while learning from professional experts about the latest research and thinking around such key issues as accessibility, visitability, universal design, transportation innovations, signage, complete streets, evidence-based health promotion, housing/long-term care innovations, and other environmental supports for elders and people with disabilities.

Following advance work designed to provide base maps, zoning information, and photo inventories of prospective sites, the urban planners and architects focused on six specific neighborhoods in which development properties were embedded. Three large public meetings and additional educational workshops for providers and other key stakeholders occurred throughout the period of the charrette, enabling the public to view initial, midway, and final visual renderings of proposed development ideas. Andrés Duany, co-founder of the firm, and a founder of the Congress for New Urbanism, provided fascinating public lectures that challenged Atlantans to radically rethink their history of urban sprawl and apply the principles of New Urbanism to the new demographic imperative.

The Atlanta charrette will likely exert a significant influence as a participation model capable of helping cities and towns throughout the United States to reengineer the built environment in wholesale fashion —creating housing, sidewalks, streets, and mixed-use urban centers that completely transform the experience of aging for millions of people.

CONCLUSION

We have become an expert-driven culture. We cannot make a move without a white paper, a traffic count, an advisor, a personal trainer. Yet, Jason Surowiecki, in The Wisdom of Crowds (2004), has noted how a collective of ordinary individuals can often come to a better decision than any one individual in particular, including the expert. It follows that, in order to perfect our democracy, we require that ordinary voices and perspectives be acknowledged for their own form of expertise. Participation methods provide a vehicle for accomplishing this goal. They provide us a magnifying lens through which we can develop a deeper understanding of the lifeworld of elders and the means by which they (we) develop a sense of place. These methods keep us grounded in everyday reality. They teach us how our expert-designed programs really affect the recipients. They reveal the diversity within a population that is largely stereotyped by Madison Avenue. And in revealing diverse experiences and perspectives, they force us to confront the challenge of developing communities that work for the least of us as well as the most of us.

ᴄᴇᴏ HELEN THE CAT LADY ᴄᴇᴏ

Recently, in preparation for a local visioning workshop, I spent some time wandering the streets and alleys of the neighborhood that was to be the focus of my talk. Leaving my pickup truck in a church parking lot, I ventured up the adjoining gravel alley to introduce myself to an older woman in trench coat and babushka, who was lingering near the hedge. Reaching her, I realized that she was keeping a close eye on a fluffy cat nosing through the leaves under the brush. She was, I realized, walking her cat. Who walks a cat, I wondered? Only someone with special sensitivities and lots of time, it seemed to me. After introducing herself as "Helen" and noticing my camera, she asked if I was with the newspaper. No, I explained, I was just exploring these great alleys and would love to take her picture. She responded to my request with an emphatic "no" and, when I asked if I could take the kitty's picture, she added that she did not think he would approve either. Helen explained that the cat was her neighbor's, who had little time to pay attention to it and, hence, the cat spent the day with her, an arrangement that suited Helen, the neighbor, and the cat perfectly. "I'm too old and could die anytime, so why would I want a cat?" she explained. Daily, however, Helen and the kitty enjoyed a leisurely and curious stroll through the alleys, each time terminating at "his cousin's" house where, it seems, the cat also just happened to have a girlfriend. Later, at the workshop, participants informed me that I had just met a beloved member of the small community. Helen, they told me, is much appreciated for her ability to nurture and protect the valuable relationships between people and animals in the neighborhood. Now that is a good neighborhood in which to grow old—a neighborhood that recognizes and appreciates the individual gifts that people like Helen have to offer, no matter how trivial they may appear at first glance.

.

CHAPTER 5

Memory and the Creation of Place

GERONTOLOGY'S FASCINATION WITH REMINISCENCE

The notion of the life review as a normal, if not an essential developmental task of old age has enjoyed a 40-year run in the field of gerontology. While the Ericksonian roots of the idea were certainly acknowledged by him, it was psychiatrist Robert Butler who introduced the notion into gerontology in a 1963 article in the journal *Psychiatry*. Writing as a psychoanalyst, Butler suggested that life review is triggered by the awareness of finitude—a particularly modernist idea—and that it enables the individual to construct an integrated and meaningful life in the face of its impending dissolution. Despite the fact that Butler saw the potential for life review to lead to negative consequences, the received knowledge today is that reminiscence is "good"—what Harry Moody refers to as a normative take on the concept (1986, 24). Hence, life review has been transformed into "reminiscence therapy," and its practitioners abound in settings such as senior centers and nursing homes. In essence, reminiscence is seen as a natural and therapeutic process that enables the self to construct its final definition in preparation for death. Sharon Kaufman's book, *The Ageless Self* (1986), is an anthropological treatise that has found a receptive audience among gerontologists and augments Butler's thesis by arguing that reminiscence is an active process of constructing a self that is *continuous* with earlier selves and not, in old age, a self divorced from its own past.

Harry Moody suggests that the notion of the reminiscing self has found its historical moment as a necessary fiction in the modern project of self-absorption. He sees its willing reception among gerontologists to be a consequence of a pervasive psychological reductionism that dominates the science and reduces the search for the meaning of life to the meaning of (my) life (1986, 27ff). Kathleen Woodward concurs, noting that the concomitant Western literary tradition also builds upon the notion that narration emerges from the consciousness of death (1986, 145).

In this tradition, life comes to equate with autobiographical consciousness and, hence, memory becomes the hallmark of thought—the shaper of self. The uses of memory become personal, part and parcel of the modern quest for individual meaning. As such, the traditional anthropological meaning of memory as cultural legacy becomes subverted in favor of a universal psychology. Ethnographer Barbara Myerhoff succumbs, partially, to this notion of memory in her summation of the narrative work of Jacob, a participant in the Jewish Senior Center, which was the focus of her fieldwork and reported upon in the wonderful ethnography *Number Our Days:*

> In constructing a Self, Jacob—and the other old people— sought to define a coherent experience of "I," a sense of continuity with one's past selves ... To experience the Self as a stable, continuous being through time, across continents and epochs, despite dramatic physical changes, is especially important to the old ... a major developmental task for the elderly, resulting in the integration that will allow them to age well and die well. (1978, 222)

To her credit, Myerhoff then goes beyond the unidimensional understanding of memory as explicated in the preceding passage. She accepts the psychological function of memory but brings in the cultural when elucidating Jacob's further use of memory as a device to promote the maintenance of a *shared* past. As a legacy, Jacob had provided funds for the celebration of his birthday for five years beyond his death, an occasion to be celebrated with the saying of the Kaddish, the mourners' prayer. While normally associated with death and memorial services, the Kaddish was to serve to bind together the Senior Center participants along a continuous thread, transcending *individual* grief and joining the ancestors, the living, and those yet unborn into a single community. Citing Suzanne Langer, Myerhoff refers to this use of memory as "transformational"—"when symbol and object seem to fuse and are experienced in a perfectly undifferentiated whole." This is the ritual use of memories—they "carry participants beyond words and word-bound thought ... at these times symbols do not merely point to things beyond themselves ... they call into play imagination, emotion, and insight ... making present the meanings of symbols known to us not by intelligence and reason but in experience" (1978, 225).

With this passage, Myerhoff squarely places memory beyond the province of individual thought and cognition and, as such, takes memory back for anthropology. Not simply "self-serving," memory reenters the social world as a cultural resource—a device by which people do things *together*. Moreover, memory does not merely *represent* or signify the group, but helps to build it, to sustain it in an active, *constitutive* process.

It is this notion of memory as a kind of praxis, a bodily experience, that has been underacknowledged by mainstream gerontology. It does not require us to ignore the personal uses of memory but challenges us to understand memory as it lives *outside* of people's heads and, I would argue, in people's lived, collective, and bodily experiences of place.

MOVING THROUGH MEMORY

I suspect that if I asked you to think about the home you occupied at age ten you would sit back, close your eyes, and move through that space in your mind's eye. So it is when I ask elderly residents of a local convalescent center to revisit, in their mind's eye, the homes of their youth and early adulthood. Opha Miller, 100 years old, closes her eyes and describes the pasture seen from her back window as if it still exists. She sits on the porch and looks out across the road at the Wisnand girls. She recalls her husband, a good carpenter, building that porch, and revisits the bedroom in which she gave birth to her daughter. Moving further back in time, 93 years, she describes how, at age seven, she lived with her family in Texas and helped fill bags with cotton and dump them into a canvas covered wagon. She is crossing a little bridge and hears a train whistle right up close. "I jumped off that bridge and the passenger train nearly hit me!" She never told her folks about that since she knew that would mean trouble. Through the irony of dementia she confesses once again, three minutes later, and reiterates the story just as before.

Another resident nicknamed Hack shows me the photograph of his former home on the wall of his room at the center. It is a small bungalow highlighted in front by a stone arch at the beginning of the sidewalk leading to the house. The arch has no adjoining fence and so does not keep things out but welcomes them in. Hack mentions how his son used to mow the grass across the road at Opha Miller's house (yes, the very same Opha now lives in the next room!). Hack, speaking of his son while pointing to the arch in the picture, says:

H: He sees now what old Dad did. I did that.

P: You did?

H: A windstorm blew it down . . . my son said [to the insurance man], "There's nobody gonna fix that unless they put it back exactly like Dad had it!" . . . this guy looked at it and said, "I'll put it back exactly like that" . . . and he did.

Pointing to the stone work, Hack says:

H: I cut every one of them with a pitchin' tool.

P: You cut it with pitching tools . . . you mean you dug them out of the ground?

H: You face it.

P: You call that pitching it?

H: Yeah, pitching it is making rock face out of it . . . and squarin' it up— it's a breakin' tool [*shows me the movement of the tool in a chopping motion with his hands*] . . . something like a big wide chisel, but it's cut on just like that—you get that just right and it'll break the rock. But you line it with a square, and then cut it. Put your rock face on it.

As he talks about his life, I generally stand in awe, reminded how I love the work that brings me here to listen. When Hack talks about doing some "water witchin' " as a kid, and not finding a forked peach branch, he lets me know with his hands how he improvised with a "coke bottle and a number nine wire." When he tells about the man from Texas who came up to drill wells, it seems important to remark that he used a number five casing, "not a number six like they use around here." And when Hack drew his water from a rock spring out at his Greene County home, it was cold: "It was at least 51 degrees, and that water in the wintertime would feel good on your hands."

As he talks, his body enters into the conversation. The objects we use to construct our conversation, the pictures on the wall, help cement the relationship between us and place us in the imaginary landscape we are noting together.

Now, a conventional, semiotic understanding of the objects in Hack's room might suggest the stone arch represents Hack's friendliness and hospitable nature. It might suggest that, for Hack, the arch represents a valued past. Of course, it does. The stone arch is significant. It does have symbolic import—as a symbol of his artisanship and a vehicle for a son's pride in his father. But it is more than that. It is a presence in and of itself. As Hack stands there and "faces" those rocks with his hands, that arch is rebuilt, recreated anew, reexperienced not as symbol but as home itself. As Hack's body enters into this process of memory, the effect is transformational, in Myerhoff's sense; the past enters into the present and transforms the institutional *space* of his room into the *place* of his experience.

Bachelard, in *The Poetics of Space*, describes this memory of the body:

> the house we were born in is physically inscribed in us. It is a group of organic habits. After twenty years, in spite of all the other anonymous stairways, we would recapture the reflexes of the "first stairway," we would not stumble on that rather high step. The house's entire being would open up, faithful to our own being. We would push that door that creaks with the same gesture, we would find our way in the dark to the distant attic. The feel of the tiniest latch has remained in our hands. (1994, 15)

Wendell Berry, Kentucky farmer, poet, and essayist, describes this bodily attachment to place in his short novel, *The Memory of Old Jack*. In the novel, old Kentucky farmer Jack Beechum no longer farms his old place. Though he lives in the boarding house in town, he dwells in the memories of place as the narrator describes:

> [But] the present is small and the future perhaps still smaller. And what his mind is apt to do is leap out of that confinement, like an old dog, still strong, that has been penned up and then let loose in the one countryside that it knows and that it knew for a long time. But it is like an old dog possessed by an old man's intelligent ghost that remembers all it has seen and done and all the places it has known, and that goes back to haunt and lurk in those places. Some days he can keep it very well in hand, just wandering and rummaging around in what he remembers. He is amazed at what he comes upon that he thought he had forgot ... Sometimes he can recover a

whole day, with the work he did in it, and the places, and the animals and the people and even the words that belong to it. (1974, 31–32)

So memory of home is not merely symbolic, representational. Rather, it draws upon one's whole being as it is recollected. The proper study of it is not semiotic but phenomenological. As the original experience involves the whole body, is it any wonder that its memory should do the same?

THE ERASURE OF MEMORY IN INSTITUTIONAL SPACES

In ways that are compelling to me because they resonate with my own experience of place, Bachelard, Berry, Hack, and Opha have shown us the role that memory plays in converting empty space into place. Important objects are not mere souvenirs (though the root meaning of the word suggests a bodily "coming back again"). They take on meaning as they evoke narrative and recreate bodily experiences. Memory, it seems, is the hallmark of a good place. We might say that a good place remembers itself to us. More properly, we might say that a good place has a kind of mirror quality because it helps us to remember ourselves to ourselves. Kathleen Woodward cites a passage from *The Stone Angel*, by Margaret Laurence, in which 90-year-old Hagar Shipley finds himself in his objects:

> My shreds and remnants of years are scattered through it (the house) visibly in lamps and vases ... If I am not somehow contained in them and in this house, something of all change caught and fixed here, eternal enough for my purposes, then I do not know where I am to be found at all. (1991, 146)

I am reminded also of Myerhoff's comment that, in constructing a sense of self in old age, one benefits from the presence of "reflecting surfaces" —definitional rituals, audiences, listeners, and witnesses (1978, 222). Here, the mirror is not the place itself, but the people who inhabit it. Memory, again, is not so much a feature of individual psychology but, being shared, a feature of culture. As Molly Schuchat says, "It only counts if you share it" (1995).

A good place, then, is also a "keeping place"—it holds people together through their common participation in its qualities. As Wendell Berry put it in another essay, "a human community, then, if it is to last, must exert a kind of centripetal force, holding local soil and local memory in place" (1990, 155). Perhaps our chief criticism of the institution we call the nursing home, then, should be that it too often erases memory. Now this may be difficult to perceive at first for we are talking about noticing absences and silences—the semiotician's zero signs. How do you notice something that is not there? I am suggesting that we think not about what we see, or hear, or smell, when we enter the nursing home, but what we do not see, do not hear when we enter into this space. In evaluating the quality of this environment then, we might ask:

— Where is the memory of this place?
— Where is the evidence that people have *lived* here?
— Where are the personal traces of former residents?
— Where are their pictures, their mementos, their trophies, their headlines, their scrapbooks?
— Did they laugh? Did they cry?
— Were they loved? Did they love?
— ... and where is the evidence that people *died* here?
— Where are the memorials, the funerals, the survivors?
— ... and did anyone make an impact here?

    as a worker?
    as a volunteer?
    as a family member?

    Too often, we look and do not see. Traces have been obliterated. Death has been spirited out the back door. The room has been cleared and cleaned to receive another. Valuable possessions are bagged, tagged, and gone with a family sometimes eager to never look back.

    By the same token, the *good* nursing home remembers its residents to us. It celebrates their presence and enables them to create place. It creates home through enabling its *occupation*, its *dwelling*, through bodily practice. It invites former residents to return (yes, they do exist). One sees previous family members returning to sustain ties with friends of the deceased. One sees memorial services to acknowledge death and graduation ceremonies to celebrate the triumph of rehabilitation (see Shield 1988, 76ff). Yet, it is a struggle to enable the creation of place where so many factors mitigate against memory making:

> ▸ The lack of temporal depth in relationships due to staff rotation, the fear of approaching the sick, and death itself

At the Crescent Nursing Home, where anthropologist Nancy Foner studied the working lives of nursing assistants, the turnover rate is remarkably low (as low as 5 percent). She attributes this low turnover rate to the relatively high wages and job stability offered to the predominantly Caribbean and Hispanic workers in this unionized setting (as compared to most nursing homes around the United States). The long tenure of most nursing assistants positively reflects on the caring and enduring relationships engendered among staff and residents in this facility (Foner 1994, 17). Compare this with the average turnover rates ranging from 40 percent to 75 percent annually in most nursing homes around the country and the very real problem, as I have seen, with nursing assistants coming and going so quickly that they have no real possibility of forming lasting relationships with patients and families. Foner also acknowledges that nursing assistants who spend too much time with residents may risk the ire of nursing directors or other staff who follow on the next shift and must pick up the "bed and body" work left undone. J. Neil Henderson, in his ethnography of Pecan Grove Manor, noted how superficial the interactions between nursing assistants and residents might be. In the words of his interviewee, the Director of Nursing:

> All of them (CNAs) are needed for basic care, so that the emotional side is kind of left (undone) . . . It is hard to just sit down and have eye-to-eye contact and really feel close to the patient when you are giving them daily care. (1995, 45)

Renee Shield, in her ethnography of Franklin Nursing Home, notes how peer relationships among residents are clipped by the limits put upon exchange and reciprocity. The development of horizontal relationships with potential friends is conspicuous by its absence, as residents who lack possessions, strength, and health have little to exchange with peers (1988, 155). Hence, residents attempt to develop vertical relationships with staff (albeit dependency relationships) to survive. When residents do provide staff or visitors with little gifts of kindness, there is often an attempt made to refuse them, sometimes with a citation of official policy.

As Shield has observed, staff and visitors often do not want to be put into the position of having to reciprocate out of guilt, nor being trapped in an escalating structure of exchange that cannot, ultimately, solve the fundamental existential problem (Shield 1988, 172–173).

Shield adds that avoidance of enduring relationships may have some self-protective, though perhaps not adaptive consequences:

> Nurses remark that new residents often try to make friends after they have begun to settle into the nursing home routine. But if a friend dies or becomes ill, the new resident learns that it is dangerous to make friends. Keeping interactions to a minimum protects the self against the emotional trauma of these losses. The emotional distance that staff members keep from residents is similarly self-protective. People-work activities, shifting schedules, and frequent changes in nursing assistant-resident assignment prevent continuity. In these ways the nonenduring nature of resident-staff relationships is perpetuated. (1988, 166)

In the end, it may be the illusion of timelessness, the denial of aging and death, that prevents the establishment of "communitas" in the nursing home setting (following Turner 1977). In "normal" life, outside of the institution, definitional rites of passage mark time and situate individuals within the context of a supportive cultural matrix. Typically, rites of separation, followed by a liminal period, are closed by conjoining rites of incorporation, wherein the initiate rejoins the cultural fold, albeit in a changed state. The nursing home, as Shield argues, is characterized by an ongoing, never-ending state of liminality. The resident qua patient leaves society but neither reenters nor fully achieves a new status.

> The illusion of timelessness belies the certainty of how limited the resident's time actually is. The time of future peril that intact residents perceive as their fate threatens the quality of resident interactions rather than intensifies them. The residents interact superficially and guardedly. There can be little chance of communitas where the present is benignly misrepresented as safe and timeless, the future is known to be uncertain and perilous, and individuals serve as reminders to one another of their present fragile security and future certain danger (1988, 208).

▶ The dementia that robs people of memory-making capacity

While dementia or Alzheimer's disease may not be the primary diagnosis for most nursing home patients, the disorder is, nevertheless, ubiquitous in the setting. A typical study (Hing 1989) estimates that 66 percent of the nursing home residents in the United States have at least one mental disorder (generally dementia). One widely recognized epidemiological study puts the rate of moderate to severe dementia among community-residing persons over 85 at 47 percent. As the over-85 group is the fastest growing segment of the population, it is no surprise that the condition is very common in nursing homes. While Alzheimer's dementia is popularly thought of as memory loss (and indeed, the loss of long-term memory is undeniably present in more advanced dementia), it is the inability to *make new memories* that causes functional problems for the individual. Alzheimer's disease is, in this light, a learning disorder—the patient is unable to impress events and thoughts upon the brain for later recollection and use. Events of the remote past may be recollected with pleasure. Core elements of identity may be sustained through the active support of others (as Silverman and McAllister 1995 have shown). Even the current flux of the present can provide great pleasure and meaning. The recent past, however, the anchor of new relationships, may not be sustainable in memory. Small scale environments, such as adult day care centers, have the best chance of supporting the development of new relationships and marking events ceremonially. These markers—these memories—enable participants to maintain a sense of the passage of time and the body's participation in a web of meaningful human relationships.

▶ The restrictions of the physical environment that prevent intimacy from developing among residents and others

Most ethnographers of the nursing home scene have commented on the difficulty of maintaining privacy in the institutional setting. Indeed, the medical model that dominates the architecture of the nursing home constitutes a virtual panopticon in which most activities of the residents are capable of being scrutinized by the powers that be (cf. Foucault 1979; Stafford 2003). Fire and safety codes, the wishes of family members regarding sexual conduct of elderly parents, the rarity of single rooms and small private spaces, the dispensability of small modesties, and the enforced familiarities of well-meaning staff and visitors, all combine to create an environment that, as Goffman (1961) and Henry (1963) have noted for total institutions, strips the inmate of his/her individuality and important, unique markers of personhood and biography.

As Verbrugge and Jette (1994), and many subsequent observers, have noted, disability, health, and aging are not located in the body so much as in the relationship between the body and the environment. Hence, our attention is turned to the more politically sensitive notion of "disabling environments," which, being poorly designed, distort sound, amplify glare, restrict mobility, and sanitize smells.

> ▸ The undeniable diminishing of the body's capacity to extend
>   fully into space due to impairments in vision, smell, hearing,
>   mobility, taste, and touch

Yi-Fu Tuan, master interpreter of the spatial experience, notes how the synesthetic experience, in which all of the senses are employed, etches itself on our memory in a way unmatched by the unidimensional memories of the "seen":

> Life is lived, not a pageant from which we stand aside and
> observe. The real is the familiar daily round, unobtrusive like
> breathing. The real involves our whole being, all our senses.
> (1977,146)

How can the person with hearing impairment, loss of smell, or loss of vision fully experience and therefore fully remember either the routine or the special events that surround him/her in the nursing home environment?

So it is not only the erasure of memory but the difficulty of making new memories that works to drain the nursing home of meaning. Professionals are well-intentioned in their efforts to make institutions homelike. Yet, not understanding the *bodily* experience of memory, nor the role of cultural processes, the professional intervention is often misplaced. As a kind of semiotic strategy, it tries to recreate home through its symbolic representation. It uses wingback chairs, the charade of a library with books purchased by the pound, the false fireplace hearth to create a simulacrum of home. As such, it trivializes the notion of home and, indeed, may have the opposite effect on the resident. The attempt to recreate home too often draws attention to its impossibility.

Bahloul, in *The Architecture of Memory*, clearly demonstrates how this lived experience of place, this quotidian routine of "taking care of everything," provides a framework for its remembrance:

> Domestic memory focuses not only on images of places but
> also on images of concrete acts . . . Remembrance of socialized
> domestic space is thus based above all on the practice of this
> space as it is articulated in the repeated interactions of its
> agents . . . Remembrance of the house is the symbolic locus
> for the embodiment of social practices experienced in daily
> life; it constitutes a system of bodily practices. (1996, 136)

If we truly listen to the authentic voices of the residents, we can learn a great deal about the notion of home, and the role of memory in helping to sustain and create a sense of place. We can learn that home and self are intertwined. That home and spouse can be identities. That space is transformed into place as it supports a sense of human agency and partakes of the qualities of the human encounter (Tuan 1977, 143). But listening is not enough. An ethnography of place and memory involves us not in its representation but in its creation. As Hack and I recreate the place he calls home, we make memories together. By this means do we create place and not merely recollect it. By this means does memory become more than cognition. By this means does memory become transformational in Myerhoff's sense, a kind of sacralizing process by which the sanitized space of the nursing home becomes the experienced and meaningful place of genuine human interaction.

PUTTING MEMORY IN PLACE

Were we to take Wendell Berry's comment about holding memory in place seriously, clearly, the role of elders in our communities would be more highly valorized. Lately, the opposite value seems frequently expressed—that the newer the information the better it is. Cultural anthropologists have noted that in societies undergoing change, the obsolescence of the information and knowledge held by elders in society can contribute to their lowered status (Cowgill 1974; Silverman and Maxwell 1987). Fortunately, societies undergoing change sometimes turn to elders (and anthropologists) as the *best* source of information about threatened traditions (Peterson 1997).

Believing that being in touch with the memory of a place contributes to a sense of belongingness and participation, communities around the globe are innovating ways to support oral history and storytelling, not just for elders but for citizens of all ages. The international Museum of the Person project was one of the first efforts to employ digital technologies to gather, record, and archive oral histories of ordinary people. Influenced by the prominent English oral historian Paul Thompson, the Museum founder, Karen Worcman, and her husband, Jose Santos, began recording stories in bus stops, train stations, and favella neighborhoods of São Paulo, Brazil, nearly 20 years ago. Their project, Museu da Pessoa, has now collected over 5,000 oral histories and is well underway toward the collection of one million stories of young people across Brazil. The project has spawned international "nuclei" with initiatives in Canada, Portugal, the United States, and Palestine. In 2008, the Museum sites partnered with the Center for Digital Storytelling and its founder, Joe Lambert, to sponsor and promote the first International Day for Sharing Life Stories, May 16, 2008. The promotion fostered storytelling projects in 20 countries, ranging in size from large conferences to living room conversations.

In Bloomington, the Museum of the Person project has endeavored to put memory in place through a series of participatory events designed to tap the memory of elders, and the experiences of young people as well. Several events have focused attention on the memory of the courthouse square. In many midwestern communities, the town square provides a key fulcrum for the organization of everyday public life. It serves as a central space through which significant official and unofficial displays and performances give meaning and form to local, regional, and national culture. As such, town squares provide a fertile field and a ready starting point for understanding the spatial dramatization of local culture.

The concept of the central plaza has been well documented. Setha Low suggests that what midwestern observers would recognize as the common pattern of gridiron streets surrounding a central square can be traced through a continuous development of town planning models reaching back to the agora designed by the Greek Hippodamus around 470 BC. While the form of the central square finds multiple expressions throughout the further expansion of colonial interests over centuries, the function of the square has varied considerably, from military (the Roman *castrum*), to aesthetic (the Italian *piazzas*), to commercial and social (the French *bastide*).

Midwestern town squares, central to a grid of streets, have New England precedents harkening in turn to earlier English patterns in which dense towns with small lots were surrounded by larger farm plots and a horizon of commons land including pastures and woodlots. Yet whereas New England greens were often open, common spaces for activities ranging from grazing, to games, to military maneuvers, their

midwestern successors function differently. Although what locals in
Stevens Point, Wisconsin, refer to as "The Square" was platted by New
England Yankees, it has been associated since the nineteenth century
with Polish settlers who established a thriving farmer's market, while surrounding the square with family taverns and a prominent building featur-
ing a bulbous Eastern European dome. Elsewhere midwesterners have
frequently filled in central spaces with that ever-important public edifice,
the county courthouse.

In 2000 we documented the various meanings of the Monroe County,
Indiana, courthouse square over time and across the experience of multiple groups (Stafford, Carpenter, and Taylor 2004). Similar to squares
throughout the Midwest, the Monroe County square, with its historic
1908 Beaux Arts courthouse, includes war memorials and other official
core symbols of significant events, local to national. Moreover, it plays a
primary role as a locus for cultural expression ranging from mainstream
arts and crafts festivals to seasonal celebrations, musical events, and
parade stands. As a site for political and civic expression it celebrates
the central role of law in public life, organizes civic duties such as taxpay-
ing, land transfers, public hearings, and provides a visible platform for
individual and collective political protest.

While the most visible and official uses of the courthouse square suggest its focal role in local culture, the Monroe County study discovered
that this meaning is not universally shared. Elder African Americans
reported that the square was not, historically, a place for them to gather
as it was for Whites. Similarly, "rebellious" or "alternative" adolescents
"cruising" in cars or skateboarding have preferred to hang out in other
downtown locations of their choosing, where they feel less hassled.
Hence, while the town square spatializes important cultural beliefs and
practices, understanding what is "off the square" may contribute just as
much to a comprehensive understanding of local culture.

In 2007, with funding from the Indiana University New Frontiers in
the Arts and Humanities program, campus and community members
gathered once again to remember the square. Scholars from several countries traveled to Bloomington to participate in a three-day symposium
entitled "Putting Memory in Place" (an anthology is forthcoming). Local
citizens had the opportunity to learn about memory projects in India,
Australia, Canada, Turkey, Germany, and elsewhere. As scholarship
should always be based in a community, several participation events
brought together researchers and Bloomington citizens. A talk in the

very rotunda of the courthouse attended by 75 citizens brought to life the history of the courthouse in such a way as to add to its presence in the memory of participants. A one-woman performance of the stories of St. Bernard's Parish, Louisiana, helped create a presence in memory of one of the most significant absences the country has ever suffered. A walkabout of the square provided an opportunity for citizens and visitors to reengage with the memory of local businesses, portrayed on window posters and retrieved through cell phone voice mails connected to oral narratives gathered in the ethnographic field school.

Since 2007, the local Museum of the Person volunteers have sought other techniques and venues that enable our community to put memory in place. The International Day of Sharing Life Stories has provided impetus and form to the task. In 2008, the annual Senior Expo provided a perfect venue for consolidating memory projects and engaging local elders in memory work. Once again, a focus on the town square provided a foil for what might be the most important element of memory work— exploring how we as individuals relate to community. Individual reminiscence can be a good thing, and quite enjoyable and meaningful for those who engage. More important, I would suggest, is the task of remembering together. Through this process can a community learn about itself, both the good and the bad, and have a base from which to construct a better, perhaps more just, future.

∽ HOME IN A BOX ∾

My friend Carl has been a resident of institutions since age seven. As a person with cerebral palsy, Carl was placed in a state institution after having been diagnosed as retarded, which he certainly is *not*. Now, at age 53, Carl looks back on over 18 years as a resident of a local nursing home (the period we have known each other). While Carl keeps his valuables in an olive-colored lockbox in the bottom drawer of his bedside table, he is still concerned about theft. In the box he keeps his penny collection, pens, pencils, and other sundry items. One would think that the box is inviolate, yet, for Carl, it is a bit of a ruse. His most important possessions are, in fact, placed in a cardboard box on a shelf in a closet of a local human service agency. The secretary in that office has shown the sensitivity to keep Carl's items there for nearly ten years. What is in this secret cardboard box? Nothing less than Carl himself, represented in numerous birthday cards, notes, newspaper clippings about him, and letters from kindly others. Carl, with what I think is an eidetic memory, knows *exactly* what is in the box. About two years ago we visited the box to make sure everything was still there. Now, my own file cabinet has become an additional secret cupboard for Carl, and the intimacy of our relationship is bolstered. Carl now tells me I am like a brother to him.

.

CHAPTER 6

Aging in Third Places

If you have ventured into McDonald's for a morning coffee, you have seen them—the ROMEOs—retired old men eating out. Of course, in many towns and cities it might be the local biscuit junction or the corner café. And despite the criticism of McDonald's as the epitome of the nonlocal, no-place establishment, there is no getting around the fact that these restaurants play an important role in the lives of older men and women around the United States. In *The Great Good Place*, Ray Oldenburg coined the phrase "third places" to describe these gathering places that seem to take on unique character as not home and not work. Third places are those informal public gathering places that, if we are fortunate, we all know and inhabit from time to time. By his definition, third places are inclusive and local (1999, xvii)—places where people know each other, where public characters are encountered, where generations come together. These places are neither programmed nor scripted. They might be the grocery store, the drug store counter, the liar's bench, the coffee shop or café. Many writers have, indeed, pointed to these places as essential elements of public life, whether urban or rural. Oldenburg pays homage to Jane Jacobs, Peter Katz, and William H. Whyte, among others who have noted the value of these places.

Though a wonderful contribution to the literature on place, Oldenburg himself regrets not including a chapter on the elderly in the second edition of his book. He notes:

> There should be a chapter on the older generation, of course,
> and not just for their sake. Third places are typically places of

business and their slow periods benefit from retired people
who can fill the booths and chairs when others are at work
or in school. Furthermore, retired people are generally more
sociable and more civilized. No longer grubbing for a living,
they come to place more value on good conversation, on
enjoying people just for the company they offer. (1999, xx)

Oldenburg is not alone in overlooking the elderly as active producers of
third places. While gerontologists have long been interested in measuring
social networks, there are few qualitative studies that bring us close to the
actual unfolding social events themselves. An exception is Rosenbaum's
recent study of the role of suburban restaurant that plays a significant
place in the lives of its older clientele (2006). He develops a relational
model of third places that encompasses their value in meeting physical,
social, and emotional needs for consumers. He argues that varying levels
of loyalty attach to these meanings, ranging from simple cognitive loyalty
(easily transferred) to ultimate loyalty, where the place itself becomes
embedded in the concept of home held by the customer. We need additional qualitative studies that bring us closer to the quotidian lifeworld
of older people. In addition to interview projects such as Rosenbaum's,
we need observational studies that engage us in the events themselves.
Only then will we be able to see how such abstract concepts as social support are actually constructed by social actors. This chapter seeks to
redress that gap by bringing the reader into the flux of a specific communication event that one is likely to see at breakfast cafes throughout the
country, most any morning of the year.

The research upon which this chapter is based goes back several years
to my ethnographic fieldwork in a small midwestern town. It focuses on
a particular type of interaction event called sociability. It does not make
inferences about whether sociability results in either social or emotional
"support." In fact, I would suspect that, if asked, many ROMEOs would
bristle at the idea that they participate in order to receive social or emotional support. Indeed, in the conclusion I argue that sociability is an end
in itself, not a means, and that this is indeed the source of its value to
older participants.

SOCIABILITY DEFINED

"Sociability" as I refer to it constitutes a kind of interaction or communication event. In anthropology the subfield established by Dell Hymes

called the "Ethnography of Speaking"—later the "Ethnography of Communication"—has been above all concerned with the description of the class of events to which sociability belongs. Initially formulated in 1967 and recast in Hymes and Gumperz, 1972, Hymes's general aim was to establish a theory of the interaction of language and social life that can "encompass the multiple relations between linguistic means and social meaning" (1972, 39). Pedagogue that he is, Hymes has given us a mnemonic device for the sorting of ethnographic and linguistic data. Thus the letters of the code word *SPEAKING* serve in the isolation of the following "components" of speech events:

- Settings
- Participants
- Ends
- Act sequences
- Keys
- Instrumentalities
- Norms
- Genres

These categories provide a useful model for describing sociability among elders in the small midwestern town where my research was conducted.

THE SOCIABLE SETTING: A BRIEF VISIT TO A MIDWESTERN AUCTION

In Hymes's model, "setting" is a general term that includes several sub-components—*time* and *place* being the outstanding ones. Many ways of speaking are relatively restricted in setting. Sermons, for example, are ways of speaking that do not normally go beyond the cultural confines of the pulpit. Sociability, on the other hand, can be found to occur in a great many places, at many different times. Certain cultural spaces do indeed call for a bit of sociability—the restaurant bar or the park bench for example—yet sociability is above all a *product* not of cultural spaces, but of the "work" of participants and thus can be constructed in about any environment, including some that are rather inhospitable. I have observed men standing on street corners in very cold weather for rather long periods of time engaged in conversation and old women sitting on hard benches in a sterile elevator lobby, forsaking a comfortable room for the benefits of sociability. It seems to be the case that, in those situations in which the space of sociability is less than comfortable, the intentions and eagerness of participants to engage in sociability is rather strong. Teenagers and old persons, especially, seem to crave sociability to this extent, more so than other age groups (granting the fact that they have more time on their hands as well). One is not surprised to see teens or old people loitering on the streets of the square. One is surprised to see a working adult merely loitering downtown, however, and if one is seen, he/she is presumed to be homeless.

There are spaces in which sociability is an expected occurrence. These are environments that are in some sense more convenient for participants—spaces that are not a "burden" on the interaction in the way in which cold weather and hard benches are. Thus, for example, the *home* itself can be and often is the setting for sociability. Both casual and prearranged visits among friends and "relations" are common occasions for sociability. Sunday afternoons are still common times for these activities. An implied limitation on the length of these visits exists, however. Visiting should be arranged between Sunday dinner and supper (2 PM to 5 PM). The arrival of the supper hour enables wise visitors the opportunity to beg leave.

During nonwinter months especially, a setting extremely rich in sociability is the auction or auction-sale. These sales usually involve the liquidation of estates and draw substantial crowds—anywhere from 50 to 200 people. Lunch is often served as these auctions may last up to five or six hours. Usually taking place on Saturdays, these auctions draw a crowd ranging widely in age, though the over-60 population is statistically overrepresented. Elderly persons often travel together to these sales (sometimes making more than one in a day). Old persons, along with many others, often arrive early and stay late. Older men, especially, will often stay late to watch the auctioning of farm equipment, which is generally held to the end of the sale. Truly interested observers and participants learn to come early enough to scout the area and pick out items for which they intend to bid. Some ethically challenged participants actually move items around to get them auctioned early or included among a group of items put up for a single bid. This practice is frowned upon.

Though most individuals (or families) will take a bidding number assignment, the number of persons who spend a great deal of money is comparatively small, though a large proportion of people will casually bid on a few preselected items. It is not uncommon for antique dealers to dominate the bidding on larger or more expensive items, sometimes to the chagrin of common bidders. Another source of some resentment and amusement are those overdressed, "well to do" who come to bid on antiques and get carried away on their bids. Most everyone has an opinion as to the "real" worth of each item and overbidding is seen as a mark of naïveté or ostentation.

Aside from the real intentions to purchase certain needed and valued items at auctions, there is no doubt that the auction is to many persons a *social event*, characterized by a high level of sociability. Many of the auction goers know each other, especially older people, though some of these friendships begin and are sustained only at auctions.

Before the auction begins persons range along the line of goods, placed outside on the grounds of the estate, and inspect the items—discussing them with standers-by. One can informally address anybody in these situations. The goods themselves are especially rich as "conversation pieces." Old things, especially, serve as a focus of attention for older persons and their interlocutors. Those items jog memories and very often stimulate a discussion of their properties—a discussion as to their worth, how much they used to cost, their age, quality, etc.

Once the bidding begins, one can observe certain cluster patterns among the attendees. Surrounding the auctioneer and his assistant will be a nucleus of diehard bidders who follow the entire proceeding. These persons have a knack for getting to the inner rim of the bidding crowd. This nucleus will contain, also, diehard observers, who may only occasionally bid on something but nevertheless stay close to the action. Persons who see an item come up for bid that they have preselected will make intermittent forays into the nucleus until the bidding of their concern is over. They will then move to the outside of the nucleus and continue to watch from a distance, along with an encircling group of other observers whose numbers may equal that of the nucleus. Aside from these two groups of people who are actually participating (intensively or casually) in the bidding activity, there are several outlying clusters of two to several people. They may be walking down the lines, continuing to inspect the items (including items already purchased), or standing in a single spot, somewhat divorced from the entire proceedings. Invariably, one can observe a cluster of 3 to 10 men (usually old men), sitting or standing apart, and focusing their attention not on the proceedings but on their own internal affairs.

Sociability varies with each cluster. In the center of the bidding area, occupied by the auctioneers and the diehard nucleus, conversation is cut to practically nil. There is very often a repartee between the auctioneer and close bidders, but such activity is not "sociability" as such. The main intent of the auctioneer is to hawk the wares and friendly cajoling of the bidders helps the bidding along. Individuals who attempt to acquire more information about the item up for bid are often cut short—as such inquiries are properly made before the bidding begins. In addition, individuals who occupy the nucleus but who attempt to engage others in friendly conversation are considered somewhat of an annoyance. They divert attention and make it difficult to hear the bidding.

The groups of persons who occupy the perimeter surrounding the nucleus of the bidding have the best of both worlds. These folks can both observe the bidding activity and engage in friendly conversation without offending standers-by. They often receive word of the purchase of an item, which has been filtered back through the crowd, and use this information as a topic for sociability. This area is ideal for those interested in making new acquaintances. One can open a conversation with a complete stranger and not have difficulty in finding topics for talk.

The outlying and isolated clusters of persons, also, find themselves engaged in sociable conversation. Unlike the previous cluster, however, participants here may be better acquainted and therefore somewhat more inaccessible to outsiders. One can join in these groups if a move is made early enough in the day—a move to ground one's participation in the somewhat attenuated "history" of the group. If this is done, one can intermittently come and go to report on the proceedings of the central activity. Sociability, nevertheless, is at a high level here, and it may be somewhat different from that of "perimeter" sociability in that topics for conversation need not be grounded in the bidding activity.

Aside from the home and the auction sale, of course, sociability is found in many other spaces. One can discover it before and after club meetings; before and following church meetings; over the business counter (though there are limits to its "acceptability" here); at club banquets; on front porches and at property lines; at local sporting events and festivals; at the laundromats, barber shops, and beauty parlors; and finally, and above all, at local bars and restaurants.

THE RESTAURANT SETTING: TIME, PLACE,
PARTICIPANTS (IN THE HISTORICAL PRESENT)

Once I had become aware of the importance and prevalence of sociability and "plain talk" in the town where I was conducting my research, I decided to seek out a *particular* setting that I could analyze in greater detail in order to discover something about the nature of sociability. I will employ Hymes's model for the isolation of the components of this communication event and begin with a discussion of the *setting* of this particular manifestation of sociability.

Every morning at 7 AM at the local Bluebird Inn on the square there gather 5–15 men (and one woman) to talk, drink coffee, and eat breakfast, in that order of importance. The group is generally divided evenly among retired and working men, though in the winter the weather prevents at least two retired men from attending, and on the weekends, a few working men are known to drop out. With only a couple of exceptions (the anthropologist and a new resident), the participants are local citizens, with extensive roots in the community. These individuals thus have very wide networks within the community and surrounding area—networks that overlap with one another in many ways. The group includes local businessmen, farmers, tradesmen, and professionals, either active or retired, and represents a good cross-section of the working community. The level of education varies from high school to college and professional degrees. The lone woman is the spouse of another participant and works in a local retail store. Judging by the professions represented, the level of income varies from average to well-to-do. (No one is excessively poor or extremely well off. I imagine the attorneys in the group represent the top income level.)

Being concerned especially with the variable of *age*, I should point out that, with the exception of the anthropologist, ages vary from around 35 to 85. The average age, however, is probably around 54. The majority of men are between 40 and 65. Two interesting *correlates of age* seem to play a part in the proceedings.

The first correlate involves the distribution of knowledge. Up to a point a person's knowledge of the community increases quantitatively with advancing years (isolated old persons often lose contact and knowledge of community happenings). The vast fund of information held by the oldest members of the group enables them to play significant roles in the conversation. Not only do they know a great many people in the community (dead and alive) but they have more available time on hand to keep up with the latest happenings. Their knowledge is not necessarily outdated, therefore, but continues to hold good. As such, they can not only volunteer information in the run of conversation but serve as resources as well for other participants' inquiries. One of the older participants spends a good part of each day driving his car to various spots of sociability. (This is a common activity for many old men.) He is a virtual treasure trove of information about local happenings. Most everyone knows this and questions him accordingly.

A second correlate of age that enters into the context of sociability is *communicative proficiency*. One of the older participants is somewhat hard of hearing, for example, and occasionally misses the point of conversation. His speech is a little slurred (perhaps not age-related) and this requires of others a closer attention when he speaks. Another old participant has not infrequent lapses of memory. These factors will be seen to play an interesting part in the construction of the signs of old age, which I discuss below.

INSTRUMENTALITIES

By *instrumentalities* Hymes means the channels or media through which communication takes place. The channel for sociable communication around the breakfast table is primarily *speech*, though aside from speech there are some not insignificant "supportive" channels through which sociability takes place. *Silence*, for example, does not necessarily preclude one's participation in the sociable context. Indeed, the very presence of speech on the part of one participant implies *silence* on the part of another, as *prescribed* by normal turn-taking rules (Sacks 1974, 715). I myself have been labeled as a good "listener" in the group—"He doesn't say much, but he's one of us." Silence, in other words, though it is not characteristic of the sociable context in its entirety, is nevertheless an important component of sociability for individual participants. Indeed, silence is an important instrumentality of communication for one of the older participants in the group. He can actively participate in the sociable context, yet shield his lack of speech competence—not give away the symptoms of old age. Indeed he *is* competent in the context of sociability, and his "cloak of competence" (Edgerton 1967) does not shield a basic and general incompetence. "Competence" in this sense is situationally defined and not an objective, empirically describable fact as it is too often assumed by more clinically oriented gerontologists.

The visual channel, as well, plays a significant role in the process of sociability. Eye contact between and among interlocutors is an important means for the "recognition" of speech acts. Occasionally, and especially when the number of participants reaches its upper limit, a speaker will find himself competing with another speaker's report at the other end of the table. The success of the other's speech may leave the first speaker without an audience (a clue that there are sometimes "performance" elements involved). In such cases, I have seen speech trail off without any consummation, as the first speaker accedes to the more successful speaker. In other instances I have made it a point to sustain or initiate eye contact with the less successful speaker. Once I am recognized as an interlocutor, though I remain silent, the speech event continues in spite of the other speech event, or is quickly but *appropriately* terminated in order that we might both attend to the more successful speech event at the other end of the table. (Though competition is sometimes evident, sociability itself is not a *performance* event. Sociability is by definition a communal event and does not imply a hierarchy of performer/audience, though "performances" can be included within the bounds of sociability.)

Touch, as such, is not a highly important channel, though, like the visual channel, it cannot be ignored. In the context of sociability at the breakfast table it is not unusual to see an arm placed around another's shoulder, a hand placed on another's knee. Such acts often serve to focus the *touched* person as the object or subject of a particular narrative topic, the touched one being an object in one-to-one interactions, and a subject when the interaction is staged before an audience. Such intimacies are not offensive or disruptive—often they are facetious. In other contexts such intimacies would be out of place and rather suspicious, often having sexual connotation.

Aside from merely *supporting* the spoken chain or serving indexically to pinpoint the object or subject of conversation, these tactile movements actually help to create a feeling of groupness and solidarity in a very real sense. Such tactile signs are obvious in other contexts as well. (One need only picture small children walking arm in arm to realize the generality of this phenomenon. And one could certainly do an entire ethnography of touching within the nursing home scene—where touching fulfills many varied purposes, positive and negative.)

A final instrumentality of sociability, related to the visual channel, and to the tactile channel, is the proxemic element—the use of space. Space, here, is a *medium* that, like speech, serves as a vehicle for communication.

As the number of participants varies from 5 to 15, certain spatial adjust-
ments are made as the group's size varies up and down. The number of
tables adjoined is always two. As the restaurant opens there are at least
3 or 4 men present and the number rapidly increases in the first ten
minutes. (I would have to reach the spot by 10 minutes after 7 AM to get
a "good" seat.) Certain individuals have their traditional spots. One
man, for example, always complains of being "on the crack" (between
two tables) but never sits anywhere else. Some prefer to sit with a view
to the door. Some prefer the end of the table. As more individuals arrive,
it is necessary for seated participants to compress. Up to a limit of approximately 12–14 the group is amiably open to new accommodations.
No traditional member will be turned away until it becomes physically
impractical for him to sit down. More chairs will be moved in as individuals arrive, and some persons will even be stimulated to leave with the
arrival of new members. The attempted "inclusion" of all traditional participants is an outstanding characteristic of the sociable context. Thus,
when physical limits are placed on the inclusion of members, there will
often be verbal and proxemic expansions of the scene—excuses to leave
the scene, or an opening of the boundaries, wherein an individual will
sit at the next table and point his chair in the direction of the group.
Eventually, out of necessity, a second group will be formed at another
table, where the number of excluded individuals is more than one.

GENRES

Sociability itself is not a genre. Often, genre is opposed to so-called casual or normal speech. It is seen to refer to such things as "poem, myth, tale,
proverb, riddle, curse, prayer," etc. (Hymes 1972, 65). Thus, though not
precluding the possibility that sociability itself has a special *form* (like a
genre) we can still ask whether specific genres are represented *within* the
context of sociability. The answer to this question is in the affirmative.
Commonly recognized genre phenomena do occur within the sociable context—seeming at times to highlight the general run of sociability. They are
always permissible within sociability, within specifiable limits, and may
serve as markers of particularly able performers within the sociable group.

Three genres are most notably represented within the sociable setting
of this third place: *the joke, the narrative of personal experience,* and *gossip.*
There is no need for a formal description of these genres over and above
their identifying or recognition characteristics. *The joke,* for example, is
formally marked by the use of introductory formulae. Thus, "Did you hear

the one about . . ."; "Have you heard the joke about the guy who . . . ?";
"Well, there was this guy . . ."; or, of course, the classic "Guy walks into
a bar . . ." serve to introduce the joke into the context of sociability.
By the use of such formulae one is able to claim a momentary possession
of the floor and the attention of the audience.

Though the joke is *permissible* in the context of sociability, it should in
some sense follow from previous topics of conversation. Sociability is not
a joke-telling session—one should not introduce an ungrounded joke
into the setting or attempt to follow one joke after another. Laughing,
at the least, is called for, and usually spontaneous—given the common
background and overlapping cognitive sets of the participants. Especially
appreciated are those instances in which certain individuals introduce
jokes into the conversation without their being immediately recognized
as jokes, i.e., to tell a story which is half-believable up to a point when
the group realizes that it has been duped and made subject to the telling
of a *joke* and not a *report*. What we see, therefore, is a very interesting
interplay between the run of sociability and the interspersal of jokes.
At times, the group can become quite amused at itself for letting things
"get out of hand"—for being too gullible toward some of the more out-
landish stories that are generated.

The narrative of personal experience: Like the joke, this genre is often formally introduced. Such devices as "Let me tell you about the time . . .";
"Do you remember when we . . . ?"; "Did I ever tell you guys about . . . ?"
are common. They serve, again, to focus attention. These narratives are
often humorous and sometimes collectively presented. Men who have
been friends since childhood, for example, will collaborate on the report
of an experience—arguing about points of fact and making sure that the
punch line is understandable. (Such collaboration often necessitates the
inclusion of all participants in that topic, when the collaborators sit at
the opposite ends of the table.) Aside from collaborative aspects, the
narrative is generally characterized by a temporary "interruptus" of the
general run of conversation, as one speaker takes the floor for a relatively
extended period of time. Normally, sociability in this setting could
almost be described as a clamor—conversation is not precisely dialogic
in the sense that several conversations can be generated simultaneously
and there is a great deal of overlapping talk.

Generally, narratives take the form of a recounting of personal experience (Labov/Waletsky 1967). These are commonly grounded in the
town's historical past, and for that reason the characters, events, places,

and times of the narratives are often eminently *shareable*, a characteristic
that would seem to distinguish these narratives somewhat from those of,
say, a Florida retirement park, where participants come from diverse
locales. The *shared* nature of some of these narratives seems to enable
an actual *reliving* of the recounted experiences, though perhaps vicariously so. Personal narratives that are not shared in the preceding sense
are more likely to be humorous or exciting on their own account. The
reportability of *these* narratives is more problematic than that of the
shared experience and therefore they are more likely to have an explicit
punch line or "point."

Gossip: The third genre to be found within the context of sociability at
the breakfast table is *gossip*. True gossip is formally marked and goes
beyond the mere instance of "talking about someone else." Talking about
people, indeed, is one of the explicitly recognized activities of the group
as a whole (though this is exaggerated somewhat by the group itself;
one of the common pseudo-excuses for remaining late in the morning,
for example, is "so that you guys won't talk about me when I'm gone").
True gossip, on the other hand, is more restricted in that its content
may not be "safe" for the group's general consumption. This necessitates
the use of a formal device for restricting the gossip's circulation within
the group—*whispering*. Whispering among two or three men at one end
of the table, though not frequent, does occur. Interestingly enough, whispering is an activity that the group attempts to prohibit, though somewhat facetiously so. There is thus a general rule that whispering is not
allowed and men caught whispering will be chastised by the group. It is
said that whatever topic is broached should belong to the entire group.
If it has to be whispered then it should not be brought up at all. Gossip,
in this sense, is seen by the members of the sociable group to lie outside
the boundaries of sociability and the ideal of inclusion.

  I have suggested that the run of sociability comprehends three specific
genres within its scope. Joke telling and narratives differ from gossip in
that they possess performance aspects. One speaker (or a collaborative
group) will possess the floor for a relatively extended amount of time
(i.e., an amount of time longer than that normally utilized by the single
speaker). The speaker becomes here a temporary focus of attention.
In the general run of conversation several participants literally focus on
the center of the table. Here, the speaker is made subject to a particular
evaluation according to the parameters of humor and reportability. His
joke or narrative can thus succeed or fail. These genres thus entail a

performance on the part of a member and, though within the general bounds of sociability, themselves fall outside the definition of sociability itself. Gossip, a second type of genre, is not performance oriented and goes beyond sociability in another sense, as described above. We can envision sociability as a kind of continuous process that is intermittently subject to interruption by various genre performances and events. These genre events do not necessarily threaten the continued existence of sociability, however, but are themselves predictable within the context of sociability. While permitted and expected, performance is not an essential aspect of sociability.

KEY

In Hymes's model *key* refers to the tone, manner, or spirit of a speech (communication) event (1972, 62). Certain speech events may be said to have particularly predominant keys: funerals are sad, weddings are solemn. As for sociability in the coffee shop, there is certainly a definite tone and spirit among the participants. Part of that spirit derives from the fact of its being an early morning activity. Not only is there a kind of anticipation of the day's events but there is, as well, a feeling that the group has a jump on the rest of the town. Getting up early in the morning and braving the sometimes inclement weather, the group seems to experience a feeling of self-righteousness and self-congratulation. Hot coffee with biscuits and gravy might be said to constitute "rewards" for Spartan behavior. With such a sense of accomplishment, the group members can both feign a kind of deserved grumpiness and accuse latecomers of laziness.

Once the group is settled and discussion begins, the mood is characteristically *easy* and jovial. The general atmosphere is a joking one. Formal jokes are permitted, as noted, but are not a dominant form. Rather, joking involves a kind of mutual kidding and ritual insulting. *Vulnerability* is an important aspect of conversation. Slips of the tongue, inadvertently inflated self-claims, and food habits are all subject to "razzing" by the group. Laughter and smiles are prevalent manifestations of the spirit of the group. Seriousness and neutrality are not characteristic of the sociable context but can emerge when that context collapses, as noted below.

ENDS

The ends or purposes of a speech event involve the *expected outcome* of that event, though the individual end may differ from that which is normatively expected. In the latter case we might discover that the expected outcome of a particular speech event—say, a courtroom situation—would be a *legal decision* (Hymes's example). The expected outcome of a shopping trip, for example, would be the purchase of goods and the expenditure of money. For the individual participant in the speech event, however, the expected outcome may be merely one (or none) of the considerations that go into the decision as to whether or not to participate. Individual or personal motivations such as greed, self-glorification, avoidance of danger, etc., constitute *ends* of an event, but do not necessarily correspond to the normatively expected ends or purposes.

I would suggest that the *desire* for sociability itself, like ambition, profiteering, etc., is a personal motivation that results in the coming together of persons in particular spaces. In some spaces, sociability constitutes a personal purpose that does not correspond to the expected purposes of an event. For example, though the presence of persons in places of business is thought to involve intentions to shop, it is often the case that certain persons come to these spaces for sociable, not economic reasons, as Rosenbaum clearly demonstrates. While driving the county minibus to transport elderly citizens to the local stores, I had several times been informed by riders that they are going not so much to shop as to socialize on the bus itself. Likewise, when shopping in local stores it is common to observe aged persons attending more to sociability than to shopping, sometimes to the annoyance of serious shoppers. In the nursing home I have observed frail elders seeking sociability at the nursing station, only to be addressed inappropriately with the question "what do you need?"

At the other end of a continuum, however, there are those spaces in which sociability *is* normatively expected. The Senior Citizens Center, for example, was established, above all, in order to provide a place for aged persons to congregate and socialize. Indeed, it is argued by some that too intensive a focus on alternative activities, like serious card playing, are not desirable ends of the Center.

Within these two extremes are the spaces in which sociability is not a *formal* requirement (though sociability by definition cannot be programmed) but is an implicitly recognized attribute of a setting. I described the auction-sale, for example, as a setting that most anyone would define as sociable as well as economic. Yet, sociability, however characteristic of the auction setting, is itself subject to limitations within the microorganization of space in that auction setting, i.e., sociability should not range too closely to the nucleus of bidding activity.

Similarly, for the early morning coffee club, though the personal intention of probably all participants, as well as the expected outcome of the setting, involves sociability, there is a recognition that the restaurant must still carry on its own business. This means that there are limits to the amount of time one should spend socializing in the restaurant, and to the number of coffee refills one takes while socializing. Some of the retired men will recognize this fact by remarking that they had "better leave before they get kicked out" of the restaurant. These men will often move on to another restaurant where they can spend another hour or so engaged in sociability. For working men, such verbal excuses are obviously not necessary, as their work calls them away—though retired men as well will claim to have "work to do at home."

Aside from the fact that sociability is inherently enjoyable, there is another aspect of it that may involve secondary, yet important, purposes and intentions. Here we are speaking of the *informative* aspect of sociability. Men will attend the sociable setting to find out "what's going on." One older participant serves as a local ethno-informant about the goings-on in the community, bringing back information gleaned from his constant "drive-around" the town. The sociable context is a very important setting in which this man can keep up with local happenings and report them to others.

From the outside, these early morning coffee sessions at the local restaurants may be seen by others as "gossip" or "bullshit" sessions. Though the context is seen by insiders as highly informative, I have often been advised that (1) it is a wonderful place to learn the "truth" about the town and (2) not to believe a word I hear there. Information, in other words, does not necessarily correspond with "truth."

ACT SEQUENCE

If we may speak of the "messages" of a speech or communication event, then "act sequence," in Hymes's scheme refers to the *form* and to the *content* of those messages. Though a little can be said about the content of sociability, it is more important, in discovering the nature of sociability, to look at the *relationships between* form and content.

Content is rather difficult to predict before the beginning of sociable scenes. There are no topics prescribed a priori. Rather, topics for conversation emerge from the ongoing interaction, given the particular proclivities of the individual participants. Minor events around town, the quality of the food and service, the previous day's activities, upcoming activities of various kinds, fishing, hunting, and boating, as well as automobiles—all of these are common topics but none of which is essential to the maintenance of sociability.

There are exceptions to this general level of "superficiality" if I may use the term. Occasional major events—the felling of the water tower, the capture of an escaped murderer, the Harvest Festival, the basketball tourneys—entail predictable coverage in the early morning coffee club. Even these more momentous topics, however, often seem to serve as mere jumping-off points, from which conversation can drift in less predictable directions. In fact, I have sometimes been surprised at the lack of attention given to some of these major events. The fact that these major events are more generally *shared* by participants as well as most others in the community may be a reason for the lack of necessary discussion about them. The Harvest Festival, the escaped murderer, etc., were *so* present and prevalent as *community* events that the sociable context almost appears to be an *escape* from these outside happenings.

Content, however important it may be in other forms of communication, is in the context of sociability reduced to the demands of *form*. Several authors have spoken of such a process as artistic in nature—where the definition of art involves an attention to form above all (d'Azevedo 1958; Bascom 1955; Jakobson 1960, 356). In this sense, sociability is indeed *artful*. Simmel, the "founding" scholar of sociability, also noted this aspect. At a very early stage of fieldwork I was struck by the artfulness of sociability, though at a rather intuitive level. I thoroughly enjoyed myself in those instances when I could honestly participate in the sociable context as an insider. Moreover, I became aware that the participants themselves appreciate the artfulness or the aesthetic of their activity. As a particularly striking example of this I might point to the following sociable interchange:

1st man: ... that thing was so thin ... almost as thin as the *Daily World* (the local paper)

Group: ... general laughter

2nd man: (The publisher of the *Daily World*) "That was a low blow."

1st man: I know. I didn't really mean it ... but it fit so well ... I had to say it.

2nd man: You're right. I'll let it go.

In this brief interchange we actually see several of the characteristics of sociability. One man pokes fun at another. The excuse for doing so is sociability itself. Content is determined by the form—a determination agreed upon by both participants. The comment has the potential of being relatively hostile—one man criticizes the life product of another. In no way, however, is the comment interpreted as hostile in this context. The jibe is typical of the repartee that takes place in this context.

Another clue to the relative lack of importance of the content of sociability is seen in the rapidity with which some topics are handled—talk commonly proceeds quickly from one topic to another. Consummation, evaluation, the reaching of a decision—these things are not part of the process or tasks of sociability. The fact that topics do not entail great import means, furthermore, that participants can come and go intermittently without disrupting the conversation, as they very well do. Moreover, this lack of profundity means that any one individual can begin to participate almost immediately upon arrival.

The maintenance of this "good form" of sociability does, however, entail the exclusion of certain topics or, at the least, the handling of controversial topics in a semihumorous manner. Thus, for example, potentially controversial topics such as politics, race, religion, and sex are not generally part of the sociable context. The lack of emergence of controversy concerning these topics is, to some extent, a result of the degree of overlapping opinions about them. The fact that radical differences of opinion do not underlie the sociable context is evidenced by those examples in which individuals make offhand comments of a highly controversial nature (from the anthropologist's point of view) but do not provoke even slight reactions from fellow participants (as intensively observed by the anthropologist). I recall an instance wherein one man made a casual comment to the effect that female nurses in Indianapolis hospitals are continually confronted with African American patients' uncontrollable erections. Though first becoming acquainted with the white myth of black male sexuality in reading John Howard Griffin's Black Like Me in high school, this was the first time I had confronted it in my own experience so immediately. This particular comment, a shocker from my own point of view, aroused no obvious reactions on the part of other participants, save some knowing chuckles.

There are, obviously, shades of difference of opinion among the participants in this particular sociable setting. It remains that (1) such differences are not extreme, (2) strong attempts to *discover* differences are not part of the sociable context, and (3) related to No. 2, discussions in the sociable context generally involve the search for points of *agreement*, rather than points of disagreement. This, of course, does not mean that *debate* does not occur in other contexts. In settings where *decisions* are normatively expected, the discovery of points of disagreement may be called for. These other contexts are not, however, sociable ones.

NORMS OF INTERACTION AND INTERPRETATION

This particular component of Hymes's model refers to the norms or rules of interaction (behavior) and interpretation of that behavior that govern the general organization of conversation and communication. I can point for example to Sacks's work on the organization of turn-taking (1974, 696) and to Cicourel's (1973) work on interpretive procedures as two early studies focused on norms of interaction and interpretation in ordinary communication.

For clearly bounded genre events, the task of isolating norms of interaction and interpretation seems somewhat simpler than that concerned with sociability. Ritual and political oratory, curing chants, mythological recitation, etc., may involve norms of interaction and interpretation that are more visible or detectable to the outside observer than sociable events, in which interaction partakes of a more "everyday" nature. Simmel, for example, has pointed to the appearance of sociability as a play form of society (1971, 129). To the extent that sociability is intended to "replicate" society, rather than "symbolize" it—as we might see in ritual, our ability to *recognize* sociability when it occurs is confounded. Though our attempt is not to make an exhaustive inventory of the norms of sociability, it will be argued that we can observe norms at work in the sociable context (and distinguish sociable interactions from other kinds of interactions). An important methodological aid in discovering norms of interaction involves the recognition of those generally more visible instances in which norms are broken (cf. Garfinkel 1967, 37; Goffman 1963, 210), as seen below.

THE NORMS OF EQUALITY AND INTOLERANCE

Simmel has noted a special characteristic of sociability that involves an assumption of temporary equality among participants:

> Inasmuch as sociability is the abstraction of association—an
> abstraction of the character of art or of play—it demands the
> purest, most transparent, most engaging kind of interaction—
> that among *equals* [his emphasis]. It must, because of its very
> nature, posit beings who give up so much of their objective
> content, who are so modified in both their outward and their
> inward significance, that they are sociably equal, and every-
> one of them can win sociability values for himself only under
> the condition that the others, interacting with him, can also
> win them (1971, 133).

To the extent that the membership of this context of sociability is one
of equals, the individual characteristics of the members fade in importance. Differences in economic and employment status, age, and even
gender are suppressed as determining variables in the context of sociability. All members, once they are members (defined by the ability to be
sociable) are on an equal footing here. Talk is common fare and everyone
should be permitted to consume and produce equivalent amounts. Thus,
a norm of turn-taking is implied as a basic ground rule (as it is in other
contexts as well, of course). Though it may sometimes be difficult to
inject comments into the conversation—given the number of participants and the speed with which topics are handled—there are no
a priori barriers to participation by any members of the sociable context.

That economic status, age, and gender fade as *real* variables is shown by
the fact that they are all subject to playful manipulation in the context of
sociability. Thus, the retired man who is not wealthy in any way is kidded
interminably about his "hidden" riches. In the same vein, the more
wealthy members of the group can be kidded about their "easy life." Real
economic status, among the members of the sociable context, does not
enter as a variable.

Gender, likewise, is subject to playful manipulation by the members.
The lone woman participant is made privy to the sociable scene to the
same extent that the males are. In genuinely sociable frames of interaction, she is a full member. She can be kidded about "womanly pursuits
and defects" without destroying the atmosphere of sociability. She is
even audience to dirty jokes and occasional swearing. A confirmation of
her position in the group (her inclusion) is seen by the fact that swearing and dirty jokes are often spoken in low tones when *other* women
(excluding the waitress) are sitting nearby in the restaurant.

Age, a third participant characteristic, is likewise subject to equalizing forces in the context of sociability. I mentioned that my own age had not proven to be a barrier to my participation in the group. Similarly, at the other end of the scale, the oldest members of the group are "neutralized" with respect to age, yet in a very special sense, to be discussed below. One of the older members of the group, as reported earlier, does not contribute a great deal, quantitatively, to the conversation. His participation, however, is in no way invalidated. Back-channel responses and engaged silence, on his part, are viable means of participation. He still retains the *right* to offer verbal commentary, moreover, and in this second sense is also on an equal footing with other participants.

As a subject for playful manipulation, age is a suitable topic, as we saw for economic status and gender. Here, for example, one of the older members may be mercilessly chided for supposedly entertaining sexual designs on a particular woman. Or, similarly, the same man may be chided for his supposed inability to participate in sexual affairs. There is no paradox here. Though the same man may be accused of possessing contradictory tendencies, the essential "playfulness" concerning the topic of old age is demonstrated. The group is saying: "Your real age does not matter. We will define your age for you." This amounts to a kind of *suspension* of real categories (i.e., those drawn from other contexts) in order that they may be playfully manipulated in the context of sociability. "Respect" for old age is not part of the sociable context since all participants are equals. Each member's individual characteristics become the possession of all and hence subject to playful distortion, manipulation, and definition.

Probably the most important aspect of the norm of equality in the sociable context is its *emergent* nature. That a norm of equality—a relationship of equality—exists between and among the members of the sociable context is seen by the fact of the playful suspension and manipulation of categories drawn from the outside world. In that world, where old age and wealth *are* functioning as determining variables, one can observe communication of deference and respect. That these admittedly important aspects of the "real" world are subject to neutralization in the context of sociability, which is an observable process, speaks to the *fact* of an equality, however temporary, of the participants in that context. (We can, of course, see such behavior as *feigned* deference and respect in the sociable context, however.)

It is plainly recognized that economic status exists as a "real" category in the so-called real world. First, it is recognized that certain individuals in the community have much more, or much less money than the average citizen. The outward signs of such differences are seen to include such things as general lifestyle, the make or number of automobiles owned by an individual, the appearance of the home, possession of a boat, etc. Such outward signs are taken to be indicative of the wealth of specific individuals. A second concern, however, involves the display of these signs. A subtle distinction is made between the type of individual who remains modest about possessions accrued or the ability to accrue them and the type of individual who too readily exposes his superior economic status. At the other end of the scale, concerning poverty-level families, a general cultural assumption among both middle- and upper-income individuals exists to the effect that poor people should still be able to keep up appearances—to "keep their children neat and clean" and "not let their property run down," for example. In both cases, with the extremely poor and the extremely rich, the central concern seems to be with "appearances" or explicit economic *signs*. In both cases it is a recommended course of action to modestly shield these signs. Contrary to the suggestion of several students of American society (dating back to Thorstein Veblen), conspicuous consumption is not, in my opinion, a cultural value for the majority of this town's citizens.

In the context of sociability this *equalizing* force is hard at work, metaphorically speaking. Rarely do individuals extol their personal possessions. I have observed situations in which persons have indeed dwelt too long on personal economic capabilities and sensed the change in atmosphere that results. In cases where the offender is a traditional member of the group (i.e., aware of traditional cues) I have observed a counterbalancing tendency—the offender will be chided for showing off and thus be made subtly aware of his offense. (His offense is in this sense intolerable.) A re-creation of the sociable atmosphere thus results. In other cases I have noticed offenders (not traditional members but temporary visitors, for example) failing to pick up the cue from the group. They either continued to discuss personal economics or showed a general inability to deal with chiding. In the latter instance, for example, the chiding was returned by the offender and the tenor of conversation rose to a semiserious level. In both cases "inequality" was intrusive and destructive of the sociable context. Offenders were given the opportunity to enter as equals but they rejected it. They allowed outside categories to enter into the sociable context, and that context was made problematic and in the end unworkable.

When it comes to gender, the norm of equality is less easily identified since the makeup of the group is practically all male. The presence of one woman does, however, allow some insight into the question. In the outside world, the existence of a real difference between male and female is unquestioned. In the male world, and in the female world as well, I believe, women are believed to have special interests, occupations, and abilities. In the context of sociability, however, where it includes men and women, these differences are neutralized by the device of topic choice. A sociable conversation that includes both sexes should not be dominated by topics that are excessively "male" or excessively "female." "Female problems," for example, are not suitable topics for sociable conversation in a bisexual setting, though they may be eminently suitable in an all-female setting. Similarly, any demonstration of *real* erotic interest in a particular woman by a man would be unsuitable in a mixed gender context—though suitable in an all-male group. It is the case, however, that sexually intolerable topics can occasionally arise. When this happens, one experiences the collapse of sociability and the giving away to feelings of tension and embarrassment. The "real" world of sex has inadvertently intruded upon the boundaries of sociability and the "equality" of the sexes has been destroyed. Sociability may be reestablished, however, in sexually "marked" groupings. Men move toward men, women toward women. In that way the threat of intolerable sexuality to the existence of sociability is avoided.

This is to say that mixed gender sociability is perhaps difficult to maintain and not that it is impossible. In a manner similar to that discussed for economic categories, the category of sex can be playfully manipulated in the mixed sociable context. A woman (or man) can tease a man about his apparent interest in women in the sociable context. Indeed, the more unlikely is a person a candidate for sexual philandering, the more likely is he or she to be teased about it. A person's sexual status, again, becomes the common possession of the members of the sociable group. They will pick up on sexual signs given off by an individual and communally interpret them to the group as a whole. *Real* sexual innuendos, however, are intolerable in the context of mixed sociability.

Passing to the third, and most pertinent variable, age, I can begin to shed some light on the more general concern of this chapter—the meaning of old age in the sociable context. Just as "real" categories such as gender and wealth are suspended in the sociable setting and dealt with in playful ways, the category of age, likewise, is subject to these manipulative tendencies. "Real" age symptoms are not tolerated within the sociable context, though there are limits to the ability of the group to maintain this intolerance. Some examples will prove helpful.

Earlier I mentioned that two of the older members of the group exhibited some communicative insufficiencies. For one of the men, this involves an occasional lapse of memory. His narratives are characteristically loaded with the names of local persons and places. Several times a week, this man will be proceeding with a narrative and be brought up short—unable to recall the name of a character. Often, the name itself is not important to the plot of the narrative. In spite of this, the man will go to great lengths to try to remember the name. As he attempts to jog his memory by asking, "Oh, what was his name . . . you know . . . ," and snapping his fingers, he is subject to a great deal of kidding and jibing. Other men will imitate his actions, saying, ". . . you know, you know." Others will attempt to help recall the name. In most instances, the name will indeed be recalled and the narrative continued to its conclusion. This entire routine and the stock phrase "you know" have become standing jokes among the group. The older man is continuously subject to such good-natured poking from his friends in the sociable context.

A second old man in the group is subject to the difficulty of being clearly understood. His speech is slurred and, I believe, he is somewhat hard of hearing. The problem this presents is somewhat different than that discussed above. His narratives often call for some sort of clarification since they are muttered in low tones. He must be asked to repeat certain portions and general attention must be somewhat more intensively focused than that normally needed. Sometimes, the punch line itself is lost to the group. The quick-paced nature of sociability is slowed in these circumstances. The principle of equality and intolerance is somewhat more difficult to maintain here. Laughing at the end of this man's narratives is sometimes rather forced. Yet, there are two ways in which such difficulties seem to be transcended. One solution seems to be found in this man's generally more passive participation in the group. As mentioned above, silence and visual cues are important modes of participation, and this is somewhat characteristic of this man's approach to sociability. Second, when this man puts forward a narrative it is not uncommon that the ending is submerged in the beginning of another man's narrative. There is an avoidance of the silence that would accompany a nonunderstood narrative in favor of the immediate initiation of speech activity on the part of others. There is a striving to keep sociability "going."

A third form of violation on the part of an old man in the context of sociability involves the notion of *repetition*, again, one of the cultural signs of old age. Often, one of the older men will begin to repeat a narrative that has been told before in the sociable setting. When this happens, and is recognized early enough by someone in the group, the man may be cut off. He is told that he is repeating something already heard by the group. As such, the older man will attempt to cut short the narrative, perhaps by merely repeating the punch line or the essence and skipping the body of the narrative. Even here, the laughter that is a manifestation of the reliving of the experience related may appear.

SOME CONCLUSIONS ABOUT AGING IN THIRD PLACES

Some of the observations I have made concerning the treatment of "real" categories in the context of sociability can be applied generally to a discussion of the "symptoms" of old age. I mentioned that an outstanding characteristic of the sociable context was a tendency to equalize the statuses and roles of the members. This involved such activities as the playful manipulation of categories derived from an outside world; the application by the group of categories to its members rather than a personal self-application of these categories; the equal participation or opportunity to participate on the part of all concerned; a principle of "inclusion" whereby an attempt is made to bring all members into the context of sociability; a principle of "intolerance," which disallows intentional and unintentional breakdown of the sociable atmosphere. Some of these notions, of course, overlap with one another—as mentioned, equality and intolerance are mutually implicational. Moreover, the maintenance of sociability entails some "work" on the part of the participants. At times, the sociable level is impossible to sustain. There are occasional lapses and breakdowns in sociability, sometimes the result of a member's failure to learn the unwritten rules and cues.

My contention is that this equalization of roles in the context of sociability is a prime reason for its being inherently enjoyable for the participants. There are some individuals, albeit, who will not accept the vulnerability of the situation—who, for example, are too enamored of their economic status to be able to make the necessary sacrifices to sociability. For certain members of the context, and here I refer to the aged members, the context is, I believe, not only enjoyable but therapeutic. In the context of sociability their age and certain unavoidable symptoms of that age are not tolerated as real determining variables. Rather their age is, as are other categories, subject to the group's possession and definition—definitions that are equalizing in nature. Repetition, for example, is not tolerated, and this has the double effect of not only aiding the repeater in the avoidance of repetition but also of forcing the older man to maintain a *current* and usable repertoire of narratives. The memory itself is exercised, as well, which may in itself have physiological benefits.

Another way of defining the sense of satisfaction derived from the sociable context involves a look at the particular kind of "production process" entailed by sociability. I mentioned that the maintenance of sociability entailed a kind of work on the part of the group's members. The nature of sociability as an *egalitarian* setting means that the producers in that setting have similar productive roles. A situation in which one person has a disproportionately determining *definitional* role in the setting would mean the collapse of the sociable context. Ideally, all members of the sociable context have an equal role to play in the *production* of that sociability. As such, sociability is a satisfying *human* activity that involves the attempt to preclude the alienation of any of its members. For the *aged* person, or any person, this is an eminently healthy environment, in a semiotic-productive sense. Even when communicative skills are somewhat reduced, the aged person can remain a valid and equal contributor to the productive process. Marketing studies have, it is true, recognized the social role that commercial establishments play in the lives of elders (and, of course, teens). What the marketing studies fail to recognize is that in sociable settings, elders are producers, not consumers. Sociability is not consumed, it is produced, and this is what gives it value and meaning. Perhaps there are more significant lessons here for the developers of "senior-living communities" and for the very definition of old age in a consumer culture.

✿ RECIPROCITY ✿

The power of reciprocity in social relationships finds its manifestation in the neighborhood life of elders worldwide. In Bloomington, Opal Brown described how she noticed a young couple moving in across the street, and she was thrilled to learn that the young man was an Emergency Medical Technician. When she would see the couple pull in, she would make a point of emerging from her house to piddle around on the porch to make herself visible. Sure enough, it did not take long for the couple to come across to introduce themselves to Opal, and she was proud to show them her pots of flowers on the front railings. Being frail, however, Opal had difficulty bringing heavy gallons of water from her kitchen in the rear of the house to water the plants. Before long, an unspoken arrangement found Opal placing empty jugs on her railing, where they could be seen by the new neighbors. Upon seeing the empty jugs, they fulfilled the role of filling the jugs in the kitchen and returning them to be usefully employed by Opal in keeping the neighborhood beautiful. As an additional precaution, Opal explained to the paramedic that she would switch on her porch light if she needed some occasional assistance (a common way that neighbors support each other in American communities). For everyone involved, this was a classic "win-win." Creating a good place to grow old required no case manager, no grant, no program. The neighborhood itself provided the correct physical context in which valued social relationships could emerge and develop. The front porch was essential. Without it, Opal would have been a recluse, invisible to her potential supportive neighbors.

CHAPTER 7

New Forms of Association in Old Age

As in the automobile industry, the senior housing industry has historically been successful through its ongoing ability to predict what consumers would buy into. What has not been acknowledged, however, is that seniors, qua consumers, can only choose among those options the market provides— that the market creates taste and does not merely respond to it. However, times may be changing. A new hint of consumer power is on the horizon. There are signs that elders in this country are becoming aware of the possibility of taking control over their destiny, of designing and implementing their own solutions to the so-called challenges of late life. Indeed, the senior housing industry may start suffering the fate of the American automobile industry as elders begin to notice the emperor has no clothing.

In Dakota County, Minnesota, 94-year-old Gerry Seldon found herself acknowledging her increasing frailty. The loss of her husband and her own stroke provided a wake-up call. While successfully downsizing to a condo, she was aware that she would likely need increasing supports over time if she were to achieve her goal of aging in place. An avid reader, she came across an AARP publication that made reference to Beacon Hill Village, an innovative experiment in Boston that involved the development of a service cooperative by and for older adults. Knowing that the little suburban village of Lilydale in Dakota County, Minnesota, does not resemble the highly urban "village" in Boston in too many ways, she knew that replicating the project for her area would be a challenge. Her excitement about the concept undiminished, nevertheless, she employed her sizable influence to convene her network of friends and political contacts to present the idea as a project that must be explored.

Gerry's enthusiasm was infectious and several individuals, most if not all older women, found appeal in the idea of a membership-type program that would, with one call, provide the range of supports necessary to enable aging in place. The organizers discussed services and programs such as home repair, chore services, lifelong learning, health promotion, information and referral, social connections, and transportation. The complexity of these issues revealed a need to partner with one or more local organizations to provide a professional umbrella for the effort. The group selected and approached a highly regarded nonprofit provider of transportation and other services to discuss a partnership—DARTS—and a deal was cut. If this loosely organized group of older citizens would provide the leadership, DARTS would play a supportive role and, where possible, provide technical assistance in research, program development, and marketing. The women decided to pass the hat and, as Gerry puts it, "a check for $15,000 appeared under the table."

Given a level of enthusiasm that justified it, Gerry herself traveled to Denver, Colorado, to meet with the CEO of the Daniels Fund and present a proposal for a full-fledged cooperative to be developed through the offices of DARTS, and the leadership of the women themselves. Daniels bought in, with the understanding that, unlike Beacon Hill, the organization, to be called River Bluffs Village, would endeavor to serve elders at all income levels and be a pilot or model for a more suburban-like cooperative.

Daniels Fund support has enabled the River Bluffs Village project and DARTS to secure professional staff and conduct extensive market research to develop the model. Several committees have been established among the members to address such issues as finance, social connections, marketing, and the service mix. In January 2009, River Bluffs Village was launched, with a well-deserved tribute to its founder Gerry Seldon. The next two years of development will be critical and help determine whether such citizen-organized initiatives can succeed.

Conceptually, the service cooperative model, where elders are taking it upon themselves to organize for aging in place, has much to recommend it. A recent randomized and comprehensive statewide survey in Indiana found that 73 percent of persons 60 and over would find some or strong appeal in a membership cooperative.

The cooperative has the potential to address some of the challenges that elders face in accessing typical services in the community—the lack of awareness about services; the fact that certain "generic services," such as public transportation, are not well designed to meet the needs of elders; the fragmented and siloed nature of services; rigid and sometimes demeaning admissions procedures; inflexible eligibility criteria; and perhaps the most common problem—that many services are available only to low income elders and that those "in the middle" are left to fend for themselves.

Some of these challenges drive the effort to organize and "vet" services in the River Bluffs Village project. The idea of having to make only one call to obtain assistance has great appeal. But there are challenges ahead and the Village "elders" are fully aware of them.

Most of the project organizers are, by nature and by history, "other directed" individuals. Their lives are characterized by a long history of civic participation, political activism, and compassion for others. While they are not in denial about their own aging process, most are in robust health and relatively affluent. As a consequence, they themselves do not envision that they would be heavy users of the very service they are designing, at least for the near future. While they exhibit enlightened self-interest, much of their motivation comes from their spirit of service and a sense that this program will be wonderful for others in need. From a marketing standpoint, this presents a challenge, not insurmountable. In order to build a relationship of trust with prospective members, the organizers will need to admit of their own self-interest, beyond their altruism, and the possibility of true collective benefit to all members. Supporting the good idea is fine and laudable, but to be true members themselves, on a par with others, the leadership must benefit from the services as well. Otherwise, the model is one of charity, with givers and receivers, and not a cooperative. Charity is not a bad thing, of course, just a different thing, and it asks for different relationships outside of the "we're all in this together" model.

The River Bluffs Village organizers are not unfamiliar with this challenge, and have struggled earnestly to devise the right mix of services that can keep the project from appearing as just another social service agency. They are also aware of another major challenge—finding the balance between positive and negative images of aging.

Traditional insurance policies, let us face it, are premised on catastrophe—the prospect that something bad could happen. This reality, of course, motivates people to buy the product. So, should fear—of illness, of nursing homes, of isolation—drive the marketing approach for

River Bluffs Village? Probably not, and the organizers would agree. A positive approach to aging is sought, one that encourages health promotion and early action to prevent illness and accidents. Unfortunately, people do not typically take action until a felt need arises. It is difficult to convince someone to pay for something they might not need. The basic contradictions embedded in our American cultural construction of aging are hard to resolve. We uphold the prospect of a healthy, vibrant, ageless existence but must, paradoxically, acknowledge the inevitability of decline and decrepitude as, also, in the nature of aging. Frankly, antiaging medicine is not contributing much to the necessary dialogue. It fuels the fantasy that we can be youthful to the end of our days. Perhaps the marketing approach for River Bluffs Village can help engender a new form of "straight talk" about aging in our society—one that finds the right balance between hope and reality, perhaps a new version of "trust, but verify." This balance might also be reflected in the service mix, which blends life-enhancing programs with down to earth, practical, concrete forms of assistance, thus reflecting what is perhaps the truth about aging, that it *is* a bed of roses, but with a few thorns thrown in.

The strong, smart old women of River Bluffs Village are modern pioneers, to use Phil Silverman's phrase (1987). Their work might just save us all.

SENIOR CO-HOUSING

In Boulder, Colorado, another group of adventurous elders pursue a slightly different path, demonstrating that the new Elderburbia might take on elements that most city planners and developers might not have anticipated.

Though not intending to find out everything there is to know about senior co-housing, I had the privilege of enjoying the hospitality of some fascinating "co-housers" for a weekend at Silver Sage, in Boulder, Colorado, in the summer of 2008. It was a trip to the source in many ways. Indeed, Silver Sage is the home of two of the original pioneers of the concept, Arthur Orkner and Annie Russell. Jim Leach, the development partner for Silver Sage, also resides in this, one of his own developments, though I did not have the opportunity to interview him during the visit. Leach is the nation's leading developer of co-housing communities, having completed 18 projects in the United States. According to Chuck Durrett, architect and "importer" of the concept to the United States, there are only two or three *senior* co-housing projects up and running in this country. The movement, actually, is so new that every senior co-houser is a modern pioneer.

As a new variation on communalism, co-housing saw its initial surge in the 1970s, in Denmark, Sweden, and the Netherlands, according to co-housing pioneer Graham Meltzer (2005). Not until Chuck Durrett and Katie McCamant returned from a Danish study trip to the United States and published *Co-Housing: A Contemporary Approach to Housing Ourselves* did the movement take off on this side of the Atlantic. As Meltzer notes, the book sold 3,000 copies in its first month of publication.

In its first three decades, co-housing in the United States was a multi-generational undertaking. The notion of creating seniors-only co-housing would have been seen as antithetical to the movement. Yet, with an interest in his own mother's needs for housing, Durrett and his family went back to Denmark to explore explicit senior co-housing projects and test his assumptions about multigenerational living. The trip convinced him that the idea was worth promoting, and this led to the successful publication of the *Senior Co-housing Handbook* in 2006, a series of successful workshops, and wide national interest in the senior co-housing movement.

Thus it was no accident that Jim Leach turned to Chuck Durrett when he was approached by the city of Boulder to assist in the development of mixed-income, diverse housing options on the north end of the city, in an area called Holiday, after the drive-in movie theater that formerly occupied the land.

As Annie Russell explained to me, the city of Boulder was an early adopter of the urban growth boundary concept, a planning model that protected the municipality from the ill effects of urban sprawl. Without the city's proactive purchase of hundreds of acres around its perimeter, Boulder would have seen the creation of a massive, uninterrupted strip of commercial and residential development all the way to Denver. The land surrounding the former Holiday drive-in was developed in a completely deliberative and systematic fashion, with the city, as property owner, in the driver's seat. Not only was Jim Leach approached to consider developing co-housing, but other developers were incentivized and provided planning guidelines to develop a variety of diverse neighborhoods and housing types. Strong affordability guidelines have assured that many of the housing options in the neighborhood are accessible to lower-income individuals and families. Silver Sage itself had to provide 5 of 16 units within the affordability guidelines. On the weekend of my visit, Habit for Humanity was conducting an open house to showcase and recruit families into a row of several outstanding-looking row houses adjacent to Silver Sage—houses fully compatible with the diverse but coordinated design types within the larger community. The Holiday development itself consists of several conjoined neighborhoods, with prominent open space and an open park central to the community. The entire development is, by intent, fully contiguous with the north end of the city and, as such, streets and bus lines are mere extensions of the existing grid. During my visit, I walked about three blocks to the main north/south artery, Broadway, where one can catch a bus straight down to Pearl Street, in the heart of the small city. The Holiday neighborhood fits neatly within the inverted wedge created by Broadway, going north, and its intersection with Highway 36, which begins the long crawl along and upward toward Estes Park and the entrance into the Rocky Mountain National Park. One can sit on the second-floor terrace of Silver Sage and gaze west at the adjacent foothills of the Rockies, Mt. Sanitas above the city, and the Flat Irons to the south.

Arriving on a bright and warm Saturday morning at Silver Sage, I was immediately struck by the sense that the "compound" fit snugly within the fabric of the larger neighborhood. While a sign designates the location, and an arch the entrance, Silver Sage, from the street, has the appearance of a series of conjoined row houses, each with a separate street entrance, some with steps up and some with steps down. The surrounding houses and occasional multifamily dwellings are quite variable in design, with multiple bright colors, and typically two stories in height. Buildings are set close to the sidewalks, which have tree plots separating pedestrians from the narrow streets, completely filled with parked autos and giving the feel of a densely occupied, somewhat urban neighborhood. Architecturally, the neighborhood is eclectic, with intermittent Victorian turrets as well as funky corrugated metal awnings and roofs. Though the neighborhood itself gives no sense of history or age, one can, at least, commune with the geological time of the gorgeous mountains, which feel almost within reach. A sense of vitality is provided by the Obama yard signs that are ubiquitous in the tree plots.

Not knowing which condo was occupied by my first interviewee, Arthur, I was wondering how I might find him. Initially I felt like an intruder on private space. The moment I walked through the arch into the courtyard, however, I became aware of a sense of sociability permeating the air. Children's voices wafted from several directions. Other domestic sounds—a radio and someone clearing his/her throat—

reached my ears. The sounds served to blur the boundaries between public and private space, but in a delightful way. As screened windows and doors stood open, I could hear someone practicing piano to my right. In response to my knock and inquiry, I was directed across the way to Arthur's condo. While his doors stood completely open, his condo was empty. ("He needs to stop doing that!" someone later told me.) This provided me a bit of time to gather myself at a table in the courtyard, where I could listen to joyous laughter emanating from the commons rooms and take in the atmosphere of the place.

The 16 condos form a south facing "U" around the central courtyard. In addition to its more formal front door, each condo has a "back door" onto the courtyard, which echoes the common domestic distinction between public and private entrances familiar in Western culture, and typically absent in institutional spaces. The "back doors" provide the all-important no-step threshold to each condo. An elevator off the courtyard provides access to the upper terrace and to a few of the condos. Save two, all of the condos are on one level, whether up or down. Not being uniform in shape, color, or texture, the units exhibit much architectural interest. I hesitate, indeed, to use the term "unit" to describe the living spaces. When I had earlier asked a neighbor where Arthur's "unit" was located, I immediately regretted the usage. Nursing homes have units. Public housing has units. Barracks have units. Units are built as identical beads along a thread, which does not describe Silver Sage. Several paths wind through the courtyard, edging a small pond and a small common garden plot, bounded by a lanai with climbing flowers and vines. On the south end, the courtyard is closed in by two or three workshop/garage buildings, providing a few residents with enclosed parking and others with craft and woodworking space. A resident, Dan, later explained to me how fortunate he was to have access to the really outstanding tools brought to the workshop by a recently relocated resident.

A portion of the north end of the complex houses the primary common space—a delightful meeting room/library with comfortable seating, an open multipurpose area for crafts, dining, and meeting, and an open kitchen with a large island that provides a surface for potluck dishes and collective cooking activities. A "front door" opens to the street and a short hall provides a common space for mailbox cubbies. On a level below ground, accessed by interior stairs or the elevator, space is provided for a small laundry, exercise room, resident storage, and a cozy little bedroom for out of town guests (including myself).

Given the high cost of living in Boulder, the high quality of construction, and the significant investment in common space, condos in Silver Sage are expensive by most standards. The least expensive market price condo sold at $450,000. For many seniors, this is, of course, out of range. However, owing to the fact that the city of Boulder required 5 of the 16 condos to be affordable, all of the common space costs are built into the nonsubsidized units. This is not housing for low-income elders, by any stretch, but brings the option into range for couples and individuals who have previous housing equity available to make such a move quite feasible. Maintenance costs are required, of course, and as a senior co-housing project, much of the maintenance needs to be outsourced. Multigenerational co-housing can expect more "sweat equity" from its relatively more robust population.

What fascinates many outsiders about co-housing is the communitarian philosophy that underlies the movement, and Silver Sage is no exception. However, as both Annie Russell and Arthur Orkner admit, communal living has its limits. As I learned, co-housing requires a solid business model. As Arthur noted, they started with a site, not with a group of potential residents. It was the fabulous site and city—people wanted to live there—that accounted for their initial success. While the Abingdon, Virginia, ElderSpirit co-housing project was founded on an explicit communal and spiritual foundation of belief, it took ten years for the group to accumulate the resources, identify a site, and draw upon a national recruiting effort to bring it to fruition. By contrast, Silver Sage took three years to develop, which is still an extended amount of time, but much more tolerable for residents eager to move in. Also, unlike ElderSpirit, Silver Sage is not premised on a shared spiritual base. As Annie pointed out for another project she assists, finding agreement on a notion of spirituality among a diverse group of individuals who merely want to live and share together is not an easy thing to accomplish. At Silver Sage, they simply call their shared value "mindfulness." Like other co-housing projects, however, Silver Sage is based on a consensus model of resident decision making.

Not every older person wants to "fool" with being a part of community decision making. Many people have done that. They have done the PTA. They have done their neighborhood association duties. They have done the church board. They are ready for someone else to take on that role. In co-housing, however, participation is the basic requirement. This is the civic responsibility of membership, and Silver Sage residents try to ensure that people know this coming in. While there are no restrictions on who can purchase a condo at Silver Sage (not even minimum age), an attempt is made to fully educate prospective residents about what is expected by way of entering the community. Annie mentioned that they have actually turned away prospective residents who were not willing to engage in the level of participation required.

Participation at Silver Sage, being expected, is not burdensome, however, and the level of contribution is likely less than one sees in traditional co-housing. Take cooking, for example. The original plan was to require regular cooking assignments for the group, as is standard in most co-housing. While the communal value of eating together is strong, the Silver Sagers decided in the early days to fulfill this through twice-weekly pot-lucks. This has continued to the present and appears to both fulfill the value while not burdening individuals with the chore. Yet, being resident owned, there is no management company to take care of standard common maintenance issues, and so committees are required at Silver Sage. There is a common house team, a finance/legal team, and a building-and-grounds team. A steering team, with rotating membership, takes an overall perspective on things, keeping the leadership relatively dispersed and flat. Annie, herself an experienced facilitator, served initially in the role of organizational development consultant for Jim Leach and continues to play an extremely valuable role in modeling processes for consensual decision making and dealing with nitty-gritty details such as bylaws. She has noted that the size of the project is ideal for consensual decision making and that this can be more difficult in traditional co-housing projects, which are normally much larger in size, having 30–40 households.

During my visit, Silver Sage was experiencing its first "health crisis," with the unexpected and acute illness of a well-liked resident. While the immediate family took responsibility for managing the crisis, it certainly led to some reflection on how such issues would be handled in the future. Despite the fact that, as Arthur noted, "we're trying to avoid the institutional route," Silver Sagers are pragmatic and realistic about their situations. They do not expect to "change diapers." What they do expect, however, is that they will be there for each other to help manage crises when they occur. They have not committed to hands-on care but see the potential to assist in mobilizing community resources on each others' behalf when possible. When this is not possible, as Arthur notes, they realize that sometimes "You gotta go."

Arthur spent a year living in a traditional retirement community where denial of aging was the premise, as it is in many so-called golden living centers. For Arthur, it was a "nightmare." Here at Silver Sage is a group of freethinking people. They are willing to sit down with one another and talk about aging. As Arthur says, "I have a lot of experience and a lot to talk about. I have no answers—in life you make little decisions about what is right for you—but denial is not a healthy thing. Aging in place is real important, then you stop."

Having turned over late life to an "aging enterprise," using Carroll Estes's term, we have created a Madison Avenue fiction that promises gold at the end of the rainbow. This has enabled the commodification of the life course and, of course, portrayed older persons as consumers above all else. While senior cooperatives and senior co-housing must, it seems, be based on solid business models to succeed, they flip aging on its head and turn elders into producers, not consumers. As such, producing whatever aging truly means as a life experience, these modern pioneers are not alienated from the work of life. They face aging straight on, and as the first generation in history to live so long, those of us who follow had better pay attention.

CHAPTER 8

Design Guidelines for the New Elderburbia

Designing a community that works for people across the lifespan is not simply the work of architects and urban planners. While the built environment is critically important to the quality of life for citizens, so too is the social environment in which daily activities are embedded. As we turn to architects and engineers to help design the physical environment, so we often turn to "social engineers" to design programs and services. Tragically, the professional designers routinely fall short, designing physical environments that are inaccessible to users and social programs that fail to reach large numbers of prospective users. Often, failure occurs because the specialists do not take into consideration the meaning of the environment to the users, as William H. Whyte noted long ago (1988). Insightful architect Scott Ball (personal communication 2009) has noted that it is no accident that architects do not like to put people in their renderings; they would prefer to focus on the built environment without reference to social use. Similarly, the social engineers will design great programs without reference to the role that the physical environment plays in making programs successful. Congregate nutrition programs all over the country occupy spaces that are dreary and acoustically dreadful.

So good design of elder-friendly spaces must be based on a framework that integrates the social and the physical—that brings together designers across the spectrum. Design principles, moreover, should emerge from an understanding of the lifeworld of the prospective users—the kind of understanding that derives from close observation of how people live and what they value. Ethnographic research and community participation activities in Bloomington in the late 1990s revealed some important insights into the manner in which elders crafted a sense of place and belonging in their neighborhoods and community. Taking a cue from Christopher Alexander et al., and the comprehensive work in *A Pattern Language* (1977), we developed guidelines and examples that could be used to create environments that work for older people. Indeed, Alexander's own guideline, "Old people everywhere," is perhaps the most succinct and compelling charge to action that we could imagine. Old people everywhere seems, on the one hand, to be utopian and abstract. On the other hand, consider how practical the admonition would be were it to be taken seriously by designers of streets, stores, schools, and neighborhoods. The guideline works at both the micro and the macro levels, for both the physical and the social environments. Once applied, we might see more park benches, better placement of bus stops, retired tutors in every school, more old people in advertisements, more old people in parks watching children play, juxtaposed adult and child day care, more ramps, wider doors, better lighting, and, a likely consequence, safer and more sociable streets.

Designers of all kinds, including citizens— the most important ones— are encouraged to consider the following five design principles in their community change efforts:

- Neighborliness
- An environment for growth, learning, and autonomy
- A positive image of the environment
- Diverse housing options
- A community for all ages

PRINCIPLE ONE: NEIGHBORLINESS

"I put my empty water jugs on the porch rail when I see the neighbors come home. Then they come over and fill them up for me so I don't have to carry them so far."

The neighborhood is a critically important concept for understanding the quality of older-adult environments. While neighborhoods often have fairly specific identified boundaries, it seems that people are the most important feature of a healthy neighborhood. Neighborly relations exist midway between intimacy and strangeness—at the fulcrum of the public and private life. Friendly, but not obtrusive, neighbors are often the object of one's giving and one may be the subject of others' concern. Neighbors share pride in the neighborhood and belong to an identified commons. Some, but not all values are shared. One basic, shared value, however, is that neighbors help "keep the neighborhood up" so that it is an attractive place to live.

Neighbors are not family, nor even necessarily close friends. Friendships may, however, emerge from the field of neighborly relations. Neighbors are there when you need them, but one does not want to lean on them continuously. Neighbors do not substitute for family or intimate friends but, nevertheless, are extremely important to one's sense of security and belongingness in a community.

Neighborliness: Design Responses

- Promote opportunities for social interaction. Social interaction is abetted by the creation of foils for conversation—elements in the environment that bring people together around a common interest or focus.
- Adults often meet and interact around the activity of watching children or pets. Unusual architectural or landscape elements can also become common grist for conversation—fountains gargoyles, topiary, flowers, signs, kiosks, pigeons.
- The home itself can be a launching pad for interaction with others if properly distanced from public spaces. Put porches and balconies within comfortable talking distance of others. Provide adequate interior space for entertaining one or two neighbors. Place certain "out of house" activities within talking distance of neighbors, yet away from "outsiders." For example, garbage cans, laundry lines, flower boxes, and postal boxes offer sociability potential.
- The built environment can facilitate neighborly interaction in simple and relatively passive, inexpensive ways. Orient housing to the street or, in congregate housing, a small number of front doors to each other. Place benches face to face or at right angles to facilitate interaction. Always provide benches in front of interesting neighborhood gathering places such as pocket parks, bus stops, small stores, churches, schools, library, post office,

restaurants, newsstands. Place permanent chess tables and seats in places frequented by children, teens, and older adults.

- The "known environment" promotes engagement rather than withdrawal. Seeing your neighbors come and go daily promotes a sense of security. Transience of residents can retard the development of neighborly relations. Provide windows that allow for passive surveillance of the proximate environment. Provide mechanisms for enabling new residents of the neighborhood to be introduced—welcoming communities, block parties, newsletters, work parties, potlucks, memorial collections, tour guides. Develop policies to promote the vitality of neighborhood associations.

- Support neighborhood use of common and public facilities. Encourage neighborhood groups to use churches, synagogues, parks, libraries, community centers, municipal facilities, restaurants, etc., for meeting space. Create events that bring people together in public spaces: pet parades, Halloween parties, card parties, picnics, garden parties.

- Provide sufficient privacy to enable people NOT to interact when this is also desirable. Provide adequate shielding from public spaces to enable a degree of personal and familiar privacy. Include sufficient soundproofing insulation in common walls. Build foyer space with lobbies and in apartments to enable a controlled transition into private spaces. Install peepholes (at two levels) in front doors. Include small informal lounges for semiprivate gatherings in addition to large lobbies and common rooms. Install landings on stairways to enable early scanning of public spaces prior to entry (see Regnier and Pynoos 1987, 94).

PRINCIPLE TWO: AN ENVIRONMENT FOR GROWTH, LEARNING, AUTONOMY

"I can just walk across the street (to the community center) ...
I have a choice. When I get to the steps, if I feel I am too tired,
I may walk around and ... take the elevator."

Most older people are prepared to deal with diminished capacity as long as they can personally manage that process independently and with dignity. These challenges call for new learning and certain elements of acceptance. People want to manage as best they can. Old age can be a period of psychological, spiritual, and social growth in spite of physical decline.

The environment should challenge people to stay as healthy and as strong as possible, while making available adequate supports in areas of limitation. Supports should not become stigmata, however. The best form of "managing" implies an ability to meet one's needs through direct bodily access to services, or when such is not possible, being the recipient of services brought into the home.

The environment should provide natural inducements to physical and mental exercise. It should draw people outdoors to work and play. The environment should be both beautiful and interesting. It should have changing elements so that each new day, week, or season brings about something new to explore.

Public works of art and recreation are essential. Quality of air and sound are critical elements of the external environment and should be enhanced. The environment should be stimulating in its use of color and texture.

An Environment for Growth, Learning, and Autonomy: Design Responses

- The environment should encourage daily walking excursions. Small refrigerators and neighborhood markets induce regular trips to the grocery for fresh foods. Friendly clerks who expect your return create social obligation to visit. Use of "general delivery" and post office boxes encourage daily trips to the post office. Cheaper newsstand prices encourage nondelivery of newspapers and magazines.

- The environment should be totally accessible while still being challenging. Sidewalks to critical destinations, especially, should be smooth and barrier-free. Lighting should be keyed to critical corners and low to the sidewalk. Stores should be small and friendly. Entryways should be barrier-free with doors that are not too heavy. Traffic must be calmed on critical pedestrian pathways (to grocery, church, library, retail).

- There must be well-planned perches to rest; ideally every block should have an elder-friendly/toddler-friendly bench (with back and side supports).

- Pedestrians must dominate over cars and bicycles along critical pathways used by older adults and young children.
- Basic services should be within walking distance (ideally within three blocks). Top priorities are grocery and pharmacy, church/synagogue, bank, general merchandise, restaurants, beauty/barber shop, post office, and public restrooms. More seniors would use bicycles, tricycles, and golf carts if paths were made available.
- The environment should provide clear but nonstigmatizing choices between independent and prosthetic elements. Put stairs within sight of elevators. Develop preadaptive environments—design for later ease of transition to access modifications (ramps, grab bars, hand rails, etc.). Promote visitability and universal design that aids those with disabilities as well as those without, in nonstigmatizing fashion.
- Access to services should vary with changing health status. Design services to promote ease of use during episodes of illness. Make services client-directed rather than "case-managed" by experts. Predesign environments to enable adaptations during periods of illness (emergency response systems, "Plug-in" medical services such as telemedicine, broadband interactive communication and monitoring, etc.).

PRINCIPLE THREE: A POSITIVE IMAGE OF THE ENVIRONMENT

> "My home? . . . It's my wife, my kitchen with big bay window, history with children at home, the smell of cut grass."

Old people and young are able to articulate a clear image of neighborhood through verbal and visual expression. These images may have both positive and negative elements—an environment can be described from both directions. In a healthy community, that image should be largely positive, as it indeed is for most people whom we have met through the research.

"Image" is used in the broadest sense, to refer not only to one's picture of the natural and built environment, but also to one's personal place within that scheme. The clarity of that picture is important and depends significantly on the degree to which a person can explore and know his/

her environment. The known environment is much more comfortable and secure.

A Positive Image of the Environment: Design Responses

- The natural environment should be beautiful enough to instill pride, joy, and peace among residents. It should include water, birds, butterflies, bugs, pets, and other natural elements in a flourishing circle that brings together persons of all ages.
- Flora can evoke memories of a valued past (peonies, lilies, lilacs, etc.). Trees should have character and be climbable.
- Pocket parks are preferable to wide green expanses. Avoid visual uniformity and promote diversity in the environment.
- Evoke wildness as well as stewardship of a tamed environment. Create an environment that uses sound to promote well-being.
- Facilitate way-finding in the interior and exterior environments. Provide sensory cues leading to significant destinations—sound patterns, pennants, visual access to steeples, public symbols, kiosks, signage, linear parks, green walkways, corner features such as sculpture and benches. Orient newcomers to the environment with maps, tours, historical markers. Use children and elders as tour guides, historians, and interpreters.
- Create an environment in which every individual is part of the circle. Link people through reciprocal patterns of giving and receiving of services, food, and kindnesses. Promote the development of cooperatives. Identify and celebrate talents and contributions of all ages. Appreciate the "characters" in the community. Develop expectations for members of the commons. Facilitate voluntarism and mentoring.
- Make food a central and preeminent feature of the environment. Develop policies that encourage and support gardening. Support small, distinctive, and affordable restaurants. Support food events of all kinds. Encourage food stands in parks and on corners. Provide mud-pie kitchens for children. Support coffee shops and penny candy stores. Develop kitchen classrooms for children, adults, and old people. Celebrate ethnic cooking. Support the continued development of farmers' markets and regional food culture.

PRINCIPLE FOUR: DIVERSE AND AFFORDABLE HOUSING OPTIONS

> *"You don't need to do anything special on a porch. You can do what we did: We always sat on the porch and talked. That's enough!"*

The older adult population of most towns and cities includes many persons who have lived over 30 years in one location as well as recent retirees moving in from elsewhere. While the large majority of older adults want to "age in place," the specific housing type preferences are diverse. Some see yard work as necessary to their well-being; others see it as a burden. Some see lots of space as essential; others seek to "downsize." While public policy should support the development of a diversity of housing types and options, the character and quality of those options should follow some general themes.

We should promote senior housing in downtown areas. There is a significant level of interest, a potential market, for downtown housing options. This housing should be within walking distance of basic retail services, church/synagogue, library and community centers for art, learning, and recreation. Residents of such housing anticipate being full-fledged members of the ongoing life of the community and do not want to be "stuck off " in a segregated senior housing complex on the edge of town away from the vital center of the community.

We should provide housing that has some essential supportive elements to enable aging in place. A service package might include easy access to meals or a meal program on-site; access to public transportation or an escort service on-site; optional housekeeping and access to affordable personal care services; all amenities on one level, especially laundry–living areas. Any facility above one story needs an elevator.

Diverse and Affordable Housing Options: Design Responses

- Provide housing options that are affordable to persons with low and moderate incomes. Affordability is improved through access to public services such as transit, Older Americans Act meal programs, public arts and performances, municipal services, etc.
- Promote affordability through provision of common spaces that allow for smaller square footage per apartment in congregate

senior housing. Coordinate planning with municipalities to enable access to public funds for housing, including Low Income Housing Tax Credits, tax abatement, HOME, CDBG, Federal Home Loan Banking programs, etc.

- Promote adaptive use of historic properties to enable access to historic preservation tax credits. Utilize energy-saving tactics to reduce individual energy bills.
- Promote mixed-use, mixed income congregate housing. Mixed income housing permits development of options for moderate/ low income due to the potential for greater development returns at high end.
- Mixed-use, with commercial and retail on the first level with housing above, enables the inclusion of supportive services and work opportunities for residents.
- Explore intergenerational housing options. Consider design forms in which older adults occupy ground level apartments and new families occupy the second level. Explore support for gerontology student intern apartments in senior housing.
- Promote development of nontraditional housing options for seniors. Establish policies and programs to support development of group homes, shared housing, co-housing, housemate match-making, and accessory apartments. *Explore adopting the Green House® model of group living for dementia developed by Bill Thomas and now being expanded with support from national foundations.* Flexible zoning can incentivize new forms of housing and in-fill development options.

PRINCIPLE FIVE: A COMMUNITY FOR ALL AGES

"There are all kinds of ways of being diminished but ... life can teach us how to approach the end of our lives. And how can I do that unless you take elder people and shuffle them in like a deck of cards, with people of all ages. Not put them off in a corner and call it the elder place."

I have been struck time and again by the desire of older adults to remain in touch with people of all ages. While many common interests cement relations among the community of older adults, and places such as senior centers are valued as centers of such interests, there is a clear expression of desire to remain involved with the total community. Watching and hearing small children play, interacting with college students, even enjoying the sometimes wild styles of teens, are all values expressed by older adults in various ways.

I also acknowledge the real concerns older adults have about losing their special opportunities to interact with peers and some fears expressed about dangers to the body in walking near roller skates or boisterous young toddlers. Hence, the community's approach to the promotion of intergenerational relationships must not be based on some facile philosophy that forces young and old together, but, rather, upon a cautious and realistic appraisal of the true common interests that can join young and old in a common bond. College towns have the potential to develop a truly unique form of retirement community—one that is intergenerational and in which old people and young interact in an egalitarian and mutually beneficial way.

A Community for All Ages: Design Responses

- Sustain retirees in downtown neighborhoods and make the downtown attractive to further development of senior housing options.
- Do not encourage the standard development of seniors-only communities outside of the community's core neighborhoods. Rather, seek opportunities to develop senior housing in close proximity to public transit, retail services health services, and traditional age-integrated neighborhoods.
- Remove obstacles to the spontaneous interaction of older and younger persons in the community. While specific programming for intergenerational interactions is worthwhile, the simple nonstructured opportunities for interaction are preferable.
- Create age-integrated spaces such as parks, which offer amenities for all ages, from lawn bowls, to basketball, to tot lots. Place senior housing options in close proximity to playgrounds, schools, and day care centers. Build shared-site day care options for both frail elders and young children.
- Promote development of intergenerational activities and programs throughout the community.

- Promote senior volunteer activities that enrich the lives of children and vice versa. Seek to fulfill the common recreational and cultural interests of young and old, such as traditional music, food, arts, and hobbies. Seek to join young and old together around common political interests such as environment, age discrimination, peace, and cross-cultural understanding.

THE NEW ELDERBURBIA: RETROFITTING THE SUBURB FOR AGING WITH A SENSE OF PLACE

So if boomers age in place in the suburbs, as William Frey asserts, can we envision a new model for the suburb? The New Urbanism, with some refinements around the edge, can provide the basic template for the new elderburbia. At its core, the new urban neighborhood challenges the isolation zoning model that defined the mid-twentieth century suburb, where the functions of work, play, education, and commerce were geographically distanced from the residential household, thus elevating the importance of the automobile as a necessary connecting agent. According to Andrés Duany and Elizabeth Plater-Zyberk, the heart of New Urbanism is in the design of neighborhoods, which can be defined by a relatively small number of basic elements: a discernible center; a variety of dwelling types; walkable access to neighborhood shops, services, parks, schools, and other amenities; street connectivity and calmed traffic; prominent vistas reserved for civic purposes and buildings; density sufficient to promote sociality and reduce criminal activity; neighborhood self-government.

As a movement, the New Urbanism has gained momentum. Yet, it is not without its critics from both the left and the right sides of the political spectrum. Some have suggested the movement is elitist, as many of the prominent developments have attracted homogenous (i.e., white) upper income, more highly educated customers. Some have criticized the movement for its reliance on green field development, thus contributing to urban sprawl, despite its advocacy for preservation of green space, higher density, and transit-oriented focus. Disability advocates have suggested that the New Urbanist design model, with its reliance on traditional architectural housing style, works against the values of accessibility and visitability.

As a market-driven phenomenon, it is understandable that the movement has initially oriented itself to a population that is higher income, more robust, and with more traditional tastes in design. Nevertheless, many of the values elements that underlie the movement are pertinent to the creation of neighborhoods that might be more livable for people as they age. Indeed, New Urbanism is simply one manifestation of a much broader movement toward "livability" being discussed in planning quarters throughout the country. It is worthwhile to dwell on the development of this broad, worldwide policy and program shift in attention from the individual elder to the matrix of community. The movement is in fact occurring throughout the world, under such rubrics as elder-friendly communities; communities for all ages; livable, lifespan communities; and others. Chapter 3 discusses in detail one of the most comprehensive elder-friendly community movements—the AdvantAge Initiative.

In the United States, other major national organizations have taken up this "elder-friendly community" approach with enthusiasm. The National Association of Area Agencies on Aging (with partners) has produced the *Blueprint for Action: Developing a Livable Community for All Ages* (2007). Additionally, AARP has identified "livable communities" as one of its five top priorities for its ten year social impact agenda and is developing guidebooks, walkable community assessments, and other citizen tools for creating more livable communities. Even the Environmental Protection Agency (EPA) has ramped up its efforts to help create elder-friendly communities through its initiative called "Building Healthy Communities for Active Aging."

On a more global basis, the United Nations has also shifted focus to the environmental aspects of aging. It declared 1999 as *International Year of Older Persons: Towards a Society for all Ages* and, since that time, has organized international conferences and research initiatives designed to increase the quality of elder environments in both rural communities and urban areas. The Madrid International Action Plan on Aging 2002 recommended "creating enabling and supportive environments" as a key focus area and this is currently being implemented through the World Health Organization Age Friendly Cities Project. In Calgary, Canada, a comprehensive elder-friendly community development project has been spearheaded by a collaborative of key organizations, and its innovative "senior-empowerment" approach has been carefully evaluated. Moreover, these research findings have spurred the development of a cross-national replication model being developed in Adelaide, Australia.

So if Frey's assertion remains true, that suburban elders are not likely to move, and if the livability movement gains ground, what kind of redevelopment might we see in existing suburbs? How will existing suburbs be retrofitted to support aging in place? A few predictions are in order.

THE BUILT ENVIRONMENT

Infrastructure

Cities and towns will increase their investments in sidewalk programs, a return to the days when it would be unthinkable to build a neighborhood without sidewalks on both sides of the street. Lighting will become a more important design feature and public policy issue in municipal planning. Lighting for security will be supplemented by low level lighting of surfaces for safer pedestrian access. Walking trails will be created both for recreational and for physical benefits but, increasingly, be utilized to connect isolated suburbs to service centers, and adapted for use by three-wheelers and motorized carts. Ramps will be an increasingly visible housing feature and new companies specializing in the construction of creative ramping solutions will emerge, along with companies specialized in home modification and adaptation for independent living.

More Intense Use of Existing Space

Former single-purpose facilities such as schools, libraries, fire stations, churches and synagogues, medical facilities, and even large houses will be challenged to open themselves up to multipurpose functions. These facilities will evolve into neighborhood "service houses" that provide multiple services to elders, and others, in the suburb. The facilities will become gathering places for sociality, often organized around the drawing power of good food and coffee. In the best of scenarios, these service houses will become "great good places" that support community through sociality and connect isolated elders with their neighbors and the world. Though sociality will be the glue holding relationships together, the service houses will come to play a vital role as information centers, as points of contact with medical care, day care, rehabilitation and wellness services, and cultural and recreational programs.

Accessory housing will add to the intensification of neighborhood life, through the development of a wider array of housing options for elders and those who might support them. Municipalities will provide policies and information to support the development of accessory housing options. Accessory housing will meet the needs of adult children bringing elders into their midst ("granny flats") but also serve elders as a means of supplementing income and providing housing for caregivers. Childless boomers will be less constrained to reserve their legacy for others, so reverse equity mortgages will become a more common tool that boomers will use to finance structural changes in the home environment.

Infill Development

Existing neighborhoods and municipalities will seek ways to develop open spaces, and even create new open spaces through demolition in order to develop a richer fabric of opportunities and supports for aging in place. Small lot elder cottages will be designed and marketed to elders with accompanying maintenance agreements for routine gutter cleaning, furnace maintenance, yard care, etc., often in partnership with local non-profits with access to youth energies such as Boy Scouts, Vocational Training programs, and others. Elder cottages will, of course, be designed for "easy living" with accessibility features and smart house technologies.

Open spaces created in existing neighborhoods will also be made available for creative congregate housing options, including small-scale "Golden Girls" shared housing types, senior and intergenerational co-housing, and domestically scaled long-term care settings such as the innovative Green House model pioneered by William Thomas.

NEW SERVICES

Mobility

Given the automobile-dependent design of traditional suburbs, new forms of transportation and mobility will, of necessity, emerge as elders give up their automobiles. Municipalities will begin investing in smaller, quiet, and energy-efficient buses that are able to make tight turns in traditional culs-de-sac. New forms of car pooling will emerge, utilizing Internet-based social networking as a tool to assist riders and drivers to connect.

Support Services

Nonmedical support services, providing assistance with instrumental and other activities of daily living, will see huge growth as boomers reject the nursing home trajectories of their parents. Personal care assistants trained to help with yard and house maintenance, cooking, bathing, and

medication regimens, will be offered affordable or free housing in neighborhoods in exchange for supporting a small group of elders in need of support.

TECHNOLOGY

Technologies will be developed to help make existing suburbs work for
the next generation of elders. Broadband access to the Internet will
support consulting careers and new careers in design, the arts, mail order
businesses. Social networking sites will support neighborly relationships
and the exchange of services. Technologies will support remote interaction with family and service providers, utilizing interactive audio, video,
and sensor systems. Acute health problems and emergencies will be
responded to through the assistance of emergency alert systems. Chronic
health problems will be managed through telemedicine services facilitat-
ing the two-way exchange of information between householders and
medical providers.

THE RETURN OF RETAIL

One of the chief absences of existing suburbs, basic retail, will return,
echoing the day of the corner grocery. Neighborhood multiservice centers will make space available for small retail businesses, even reinventing
the live-above-the-shop lifestyle of past years. In addition to serving
walk-in customers, big box stores such as Wal-Mart, Costco, etc., will
develop services to deliver specialized orders to neighborhood service
centers, with individual customers utilizing the Internet for the assem-
blage of household shopping lists and the creation of collective neighborhood orders.

In the early years of the American suburb, the one-car family meant
that the "little woman" found herself homebound, isolated from services.
The hucksters, the Jewel Tea man, the Fuller Brush man all stepped forward to provide a convenient array of products and services in the
convenience of the home. Will we not see a renaissance of these services
providing valuable supports and access to retail products by those elders
similarly homebound by their lack of automobile independence?

HOW WILL IT HAPPEN?

If, as usually happens in the United States, the market is expected to be
the solution to the future needs of Elderburbia, we would expect these

innovations to appear first in more affluent communities, with sufficient economies of scale to enable mass customization. The trend is perhaps already evident with the success of such franchise operations as Home Instead, a very successful national provider of nonmedical support services. Elders themselves, where the finances and numbers are sufficient, might develop new collectives to engage in group purchasing of goods and services for their neighborhoods, as described in Chapter 6. If consumerism, devolution, and privatization is the model for the future Elderburb, we can also assume that the value of individual consumer choice will guide the development of new products and services. Rather than seeing uniform solutions to the housing needs of elders, for example, we will see the development of multiple niche markets with specialized products, but serving national audiences to achieve economy of scale, as with the Green House model, for example.

With innovations initially serving the more affluent, we can anticipate that lower income boomers will demand that the same ingenuities infuse the development of publicly funded programs—a second wave of change helping create livable communities for those less able to accumulate the resources to support a good old age. We might anticipate, as well, that the evidence supporting the effectiveness of these innovations will be a necessary foundation for their widespread expansion through public policy and funding, itself a harbinger of future research agendas for the academy.

FROM AGING IN PLACE TO AGING IN COMMUNITY

One leading edge development among aging boomers is the "aging in community" movement. Pioneers of the movement are promoting an open dialogue about the meaning of aging and old age, suggesting we need to be more conscious of our own aging process and more intentional about the kinds of communities in which we see ourselves growing old. This philosophy has drawn together groups of like-minded boomers and elders to explore the creation of a new life-course/life-space model, sometimes intergenerational in approach. The co-housing movement is perhaps the most obvious concrete manifestation of this vision of *eldertopia* (Bill Thomas's phrase).

Yet, as Jennie Keith has noted (2009), citing multiple examples in the ethnography of age-segregated communities, it is common to observe the emergence of community whenever people come together with both common background characteristics (membership in an age cohort being one) and common challenges (see also McHugh and Mings 1996).

Community is likely more often an emergent phenomenon than an intentional one. While the new aging in community movement attracts elders and boomers to intentionally develop new forms of community, it is likely that elders will form community wherever they happen to find themselves.

Many have commented that boomers engage in their own forms of denial around the issues of aging, complicated by the ambiguous status of old age as a category of our experience. Marketers to the boomer population are trapped in a curious paradox. They have to segment the population by age, implicitly reinforcing the subject while simultaneously portraying age as something to be dreaded and avoided (relative to physical changes), or celebrated as a new form of freedom and leisure (relative to lifestyle and location). Perhaps the increasing focus on aging as a phenomenon of place, rather than time, will provide the necessary framework for resolving these ambiguities and, indeed, lead to the creation of good places for boomers to grow old.

CHAPTER 9

Owning Up: A First-Person Perspective on Aging and Place

On a Sunday afternoon in late October 1978 my wife and I sat with Haidee Franzmann in the parlor of her 1845 farmhouse outside of Bloomington, Indiana. At age 85 and experiencing some frailty, she had offered her house for sale, with plans to move down the road to join her grandniece. That evening we called Haidee with an offer to purchase. Having recently finished my dissertation in cultural anthropology, we had decided to stay put in Bloomington and nurture our careers in this wonderful southern Indiana college town. It meant passing up the dubious opportunity for aca-demic gypsyhood presented by the offer of a one-year assistant professorship at Southeast Kansas State University. Not entirely enamored by the pros-pect of an academic career anyway, the choice was not difficult.

Two friends, folklorists Henry Glassie and Warren Roberts, explained to us that we had purchased an unusual vernacular house—a two-story, brick double pen, with gable end chimneys, two rooms down and two up, and no central hall as in more formal Federal houses of the time. Pointing to burn marks on some of the brick, Henry suggested the brick had likely been made from clay on the site. The Flemish bond brick pattern on the front of the house was evidence that it predated 1850.

Haidee was a Ward, the granddaughter of Rufus Ward, who purchased the house in 1855. Hence, upon discovering a brick on the south side of the house with the initials A. W. clearly inscribed, I assumed that this was the mischievous work of Austin, or perhaps Albert, Ward, whom I knew was still around. Years later, accompanied by my second daughter, aged 10, I visited with Albert Ward, then in his nineties, to inquire about the mysterious initials.

"Did you know that someone carved the initials A. W. in a brick on the south side of the house?" I inquired of Mr. Ward. "I expect so, probably me," he remarked, then added, "But did you also see the pellet holes on that side of the house?" "No, I don't think so," I replied. My daughter Abby corrected me. "Dad, that's where the cricket lives." Albert elaborated with a story.

When he was a young boy, around the summer of 1918, Albert's parents left him at the old house with his grandparents while they traveled to see the California Wards. During that time Albert's grandpa, Thomas Jefferson Ward, finally got fed up with the chimney swallows constantly trying to nest in the roof. He brought his 12 gauge shotgun to bear, but lost control and blasted the side of the house with pellets, an event I suspect others found quite amusing at the time. Sadly, Albert's mother later contracted typhus from the well across the road and died in the same house. Albert's father moved on to Indianapolis and Albert stayed on with his grandparents. A few years later, with her marriage to John Franzmann, Haidee took ownership of the house, providing a life estate for the old folks. John and Haidee, in subsequent years, undertook what used to be called "modernizing" the house, meaning indoor plumbing and knob-and-tube wiring.

Upon returning home from our visit with Mr. Ward, Abby and I quickly returned to the wall to examine the damage done 80 years earlier, repaired somewhat poorly with off-color mortar. Sure enough, the little buckshot holes were still visible. And, I should add, the swallows still find creative ways into the attic.

Today, as I write, I sit in the front parlor of that house, warmed by the fireplace that has warmed others for 163 years. I often imagine the Wards in this place. In a letter from cousin Ida Stout to Haidee in 1930, she remembered her grandfather Rufus as a blond, somewhat proud fellow, caught arranging his hair in the mirror upstairs. Rufus was a country doctor, apprenticed as a young man to a physician in Franklin, Indiana, then returning to the northeast side of Bloomington in the mid-1850s. He was only 55 years old when he died from pneumonia following a house call in his buggy in the dead of winter. While I do not see ghosts, I often feel the presence of these predecessors as I sit in a reflective mode.

As I sit here and reflect, I hear the nail guns outside as two young fellows frame our latest addition to the house, a workshop and what may, or may not, be a mother-in-law suite. So, despite its venerable status, the house is not stuck in time. It has changed before and will change again. Each generation that has lived here, including mine, has left its dents, its traces. It is this physical impression that marks its habitation, and contributes to my sense of place.

A few months ago I had the privilege of spending a weekend with the residents of Silver Sage Co-housing, in Boulder, Colorado. The hospitality provided to me was wonderful, and I had the opportunity to hear about the explicit co-housing philosophy that guided the development of the little community of 16 households. It is a philosophy I respect highly, grounded in communitarian values that stress both individual responsibility and freedom and the benefits of collective action. Residents were quite articulate in their description of the benefits as well as the challenges of this democracy with a small "d." I found the arguments compelling in the abstract, but was not sure how they contributed to the development of a sense of place. In the end, they do, as described in Chapter 7. But what attuned me to the importance of a physical connection to place was a conversation with one resident in particular. He was actually lukewarm on the co-housing philosophy and had even considered moving into a traditional retirement community with his wife. But, as he described his job of moving snow from the upstairs terrace and the month-long battle with city planners to denote a parking space for loading only, his body and his speech became animated with the energy of that physical investment in the place. In his apartment, he proudly demonstrated the loft he designed for visiting grandkids and noted with a grin what he considered design errors made by the architect.

Despite our lofty intentions to create fantasy places for aging, the meaning of a place, as William H. Whyte would aver, is made by the users, not the planners. This book has looked at the issue from both directions. It prescribes methods to design good places in which to grow old while describing the ordinary means by which old people make sense of place and create home for themselves, sometimes to the frustration of the experts.

What are the lessons to be learned, then, for us as aging individuals and for us as a society that strives to improve the environment for all living things? Let me begin with the former.

MY STORY OF AGING

I cannot escape my environment. As I sit here with my elbows on the table, I am conscious of the pressure exerted on the bone by the weight of my arms and the hard surface they touch. For the very old and bedbound, this pressure can become a life and death matter. Pressure sores, untreated, have led to many deaths in long-term care facilities. For me, it is remediable. I can lift my elbows and, temporarily at least, spring free of the chords of gravity. In the long run, however, gravity wins out. Entropy rules. Things fall apart. As aging persons, the relationship we maintain with our environment begins to favor the latter. M. Powell Lawton, the father of this perspective, called it his "environmental docility hypothesis." As we age, the balance between individual capability and environmental press changes. Yet, the relationship is not so simple, as Powell Lawton wisely noted. Sometimes, our individual capability outstrips the press of the environment. We are not challenged enough! The Chapter 1 example of Naomi and her "electric chair" stands out as an important lesson. She unplugged the chair for fear she would become too dependent on it. She feared fostering her own dependency.

So as an aging individual I shall seek to create an environment that provides an adequate challenge to my physical, emotional, mental, and social self. The challenge will require me to stretch my muscles, and not just the physical ones. I will certainly fall short from time to time but constantly seek a degree of homeostasis where the forces are in a dynamic balance. Over time, homeostasis may occur at an increasingly lower level, but I will see this as a natural consequence and the privilege of my own mortality. I suspect I will not go willingly, yet I will not emulate the not-so-enviable lifestyle of Dylan Thomas and rage against the dying of the light. How could I not see life as an incredible gift from my ancestors, despite its painful moments? The alternative is nonexistence, though I realize I have spent and will spend a helluva lot more time as nonexistent!

On Physical Aging

I knew the exact moment my softball days were over. That last bat, I grounded to third, requiring a superhuman effort to reach first base before the ball. About three-fourths down the base path, wham! My groin felt like it ripped open and I was truly thankful to be out at first. Limping to the bench, I watched the rest of the game from the sidelines. Once home, I removed my clothing to see what looked like a purple diaper covering my entire midsection from hip to hip—blood under the skin. In a couple of weeks I was pretty much healed but knew my fate was sealed fast to the bench and the bleachers for all time. How wonderful it was, however, to spend several subsequent years playing vicariously through my daughters, who were pretty decent softball players themselves.

I suppose it is a weekend warrior thing. I admit to a competitive streak. I would say it is a guy thing also, except that both my daughters and recent, wonderful political history prove me wrong on that. So I have taken up golf, a bit less strenuous but as competitive in a lighthearted way. In fact, my primary opponent in golf is myself and that is one reason I think I like the game. I can always strive for a better score, especially given where I have started. My grandson Jayden calls this his "personal best," and it is a good guideline for the body as I age.

Cicero, about 2,000 years ago, made a similar point in "De Senectute." He had observed a famous wrestler's career decline and noted the athlete's inability to come to emotional terms with his failure. Moderation, suggested Cicero, is the key to psychological health in the face of physical decline. This provides the balance that one needs to achieve life satisfaction in one's later years.

Appetites of all kinds, strangely, do not seem to abate as I age. Some appetites are fulfilled only too easily and others not so, shall I say, readily. I do not have a solid answer as to how this relates to sense of place, except to say that the environments in which my appetites are fulfilled or not are filled with delightfully accepting people who make the experience worthwhile, whatever transpires. While I will abstain from further dwelling on the more personal appetites, this issue of food merits some reflection.

I find that when I give too much precedence to the foodstuff itself, including those that involve imbibing, I am ignoring the potentially beneficial role that my environment can play in creating an enjoyable experience. I am ignoring the place where food and drink enter my life. When the activity is solitary, and a game on television is not company, I overindulge. When the activity is social, for the most part, the shared nature of the experience allows me to achieve enjoyment and satiety with fewer calories. As I am owning up, I should admit that this rule does not seem to apply when our foursome goes for post-links steak and beer!

Purchasing and eating local foods makes sense from an environmental standpoint, we all recognize. Beyond that, however, our relationship with local foods surely contributes to our sense of place. For many, this experience starts in a personal relationship with the soil itself. I am not a vegetable gardener, but benefit from the bounty others produce locally and have observed conversations about local soils and the best varieties they produce, of tomatoes, peppers, squashes, etc. This sense of local place also becomes embedded in a local sense of time, as gardeners discuss our unpredictable frost-free dates and the pros and cons of our (famously confusing) Indiana time zones.

Beyond the soil, local food enters into the network of social relation-ships sustained in neighborhoods, as older and younger gardeners exchange tips and foodstuffs, and as acquaintances and friendships are renewed weekly at the incredible Bloomington farmers' markets.

Increasingly, local restaurants are profiling local foods in their menus and their publicity. The social dining experience thus intensifies a connection to place as friends exchange comments and criticisms over the table.

Lastly, food plays a central role, obviously, in the multitude of orga-nized and ad hoc group events that occur throughout the community nearly every day of the week. Homemade dishes are provided to individ-uals and families coping with illness and grief. Potluck dinners remain ubiquitous at club events and workplace gatherings. Foods from through-out the world are shared at diversity events that bring together students and longtime residents. Senior discount nights at local eateries bring together old friends for laughter and the latest news.

Is the important role of food recognized in aging public policy and prac-tice? Perhaps, but only to a degree. The original Older Americans Act certainly recognized the social value of food in assuring that access to Title III-C nutrition sites would be age-based and not needs-based. Yet, only in the past few years have nutrition providers truly realized the potential for food to play a centralizing role in creating community and a sense of place among elders. The Mather's More than a Café project, originating in Chicago, represents a progressive step forward in creating environments for elders that go far beyond the church basement, folding chair, six-foot plastic table model of service.

On Emotions and Aging

As I age, I experience a curious paradox in my emotional life. At times I feel my emotions are barely in check. I regularly tear up at what some might see as the sappiest moments in the latest popular films or television shows. I break up every time Kevin Costner's dad returns to the Field of Dreams and they "have a catch." At other times I am surprised by my emotional crust. I do not know how I got through a personally delivered eulogy at my mother's memorial service without crying. The expression of emotion, I think, is place-based. A real place and its circumstance (literally, how we stand in it) calls out appropriate emotions, whether it be pain, joy, awe, or fear.

My mother was a simply wonderful woman. A very accomplished woman of catholic interests, her last years were characterized by grit and grace in the face of widowhood, frailty, and macular degeneration. At 88 she was quite prepared to die, while fully enjoying life and maintaining a courteous equanimity around others. In her last two years she endured acute back pain and a diagnosis of breast cancer, only to emerge unscathed from a vertebral surgical procedure and a lumpectomy. Though coping with congestive heart failure for several years, she finally found her match with an acute brain ische- mia of some kind, resulting in an admission to the long-term care facility of her retirement community in Bloomington. One day before lapsing into a coma, she had successfully disarmed her bed alert so she could quickly scuttle with her walker into the bathroom when needed. She also assisted her room- mate in violating the world order of bed alerts. Given her survival instincts, we were surprised by the overnight downturn in her status. Three days later, she expired, having previously decided to eschew heroic measures that might otherwise have been taken to extend her life. My sister, my brother, and our families took turns to be with her as her breathing became more labored. I happened by chance to be alone with her, holding her hand as her breath became indiscernible. I felt pain, for sure, but also gratitude for the gift of being present at the end. Her roommate, so gracious and kind, remained quiet on the other side of the curtain as I whispered good-bye to my mother. I am certain she knew, and understood what was happening. My brother, having left only a few minutes earlier, was the first to return. His words sig- naled our joint new state in life, "Now we are orphans." It seemed a fitting way to note our communal experience.

At the memorial service I wondered ahead whether I could hold up. Writing the eulogy brought tears. Speaking it brought strength, and I attribute this to the challenges of the place and the circumstances of our collective presence. Gathered there with a hundred friends and family in the airy light of the Unitarian Church sanctuary, the only emotion pos- sible was painful joy—I do not think the English language has a word for it. It is a thing we feel deeply when we lose something we love while hav- ing been so privileged to have it in the first place. Perhaps we do have a word for it—life.

On Mental Health, Aging, and Reminiscence

On this crying at the drop of a hat thing . . . it is not that I am crying in public a lot. It is much more likely to happen in a dark theater or in the privacy of my own home. The relationship between the expression of emotion and home has been touched upon by the eminent Japanese psychiatrist Takeo Doi. His fascinating book *The Anatomy of Dependence* (1971) is an exegesis of the Japanese term *amaeru* (nominalized as *amae*). He suggests that there exist certain interpersonal relationships, within the family and home in particular, where dependence on the other is neither embarrassing nor stigmatized. This dependence may manifest in the provision of care, as we usually imagine, but also in the simple act of "letting down one's hair" and acting childishly and playfully. Notably, in contrast to Western culture, dependence can be manifested at all points along the life cycle, where circumstances allow, and is not restricted to the beginning and the end of life. Dependence, in other words, is a phenomenon of place and not of time. This may be a useful lesson for a society that dreads old age and its presumed inevitable decrepitude and decline.

Perhaps we might reconceptualize the ideal therapeutic relationship as a phenomenon of shared place. This, I feel, is what occurred when I felt right about the counseling I provided to older adult clients of the local community mental health center, where I worked for 14 years. Often, the content of our sessions, both group and individual, turned to reminiscence about place—both negatively and positively recalled.

I remember the 83-year-old man who showed up at emergency service with a clinical depression that suddenly surfaced from nowhere. He was confused as to the cause until he described, in vivid detail, sitting on his front porch waiting for his mother to return from purchasing eggs at the store. She never returned. The pain had been submerged for over 75 years until the opportunity availed itself to revisit that place with a caring other. The catharsis that emerged in our session was palpable.

I remember 80+-year-old Selma and our totally enjoyable "virtual" revisits to the Monroe County hills and hollers where she and her husband built their small house and captured salamanders to sell to the university biology department. When we achieved "amae," perhaps what Martin Buber would call an I-Thou relationship, she shared with me the story of her very strict preacher father and his reaction to her errant behavior. She had made the unforgivable error of getting pregnant but lost what were twins through a spontaneous abortion. Her father, to teach her a lesson, made her watch as he threw the fetuses into the living room coal stove. Decades later, revisiting that place with an understanding other, despite the pain, proved immensely therapeutic. Never having shared that story with another, she offered to me the gift of pure communion. Her mood lifted after that and I came to see the meaning of Wendell Berry's comment that "community is the smallest unit of health" (1995, 90).

Perhaps no other client of mine found so much solace in revisiting the place of his childhood than Clovis. What was remarkable about my old client qua friend was his depth of attention to his past and his genuine obsession with life review, captured on audiotapes provided to me by his kind widow. And what I find remarkable about the six hours of audiotape I possess is that they were produced by a man completely alone in his room, door closed, speaking into a microphone, like Samuel Beckett's Krapp, and unprovoked by the interviewer, so ubiquitous in most life history studies as an external condition of remembering.

So, provoked myself to remember my friend as a condition of this writing, I recalled his having spent much time in his room with his tape recorder, mostly taping old-time, country, and gospel songs from the radio and then assembling, or mixing to create single thematic tapes. I knew that he had provided commentary on the tapes and suspected he had created some tapes of his own memories. I phoned his widow, with whom I had intermittent contact since his funeral five years previous and inquired as to the availability of his tapes for my research. Graciously, she invited me to visit and took me to his room, which I found completely unchanged since his death—not a thing moved from the closet nor bureau, though clean and tidy as a pin, as is always the case with her entire house. Atop the bureau, among numerous family pictures, sat his wooden, slotted case, holding perhaps 100 or more audiocassettes, carefully labeled with dates and themes. Sure enough, there were five tapes labeled *Golden Memories*, and I suspected these contained his personal memories. With her permission, I borrowed the tapes to duplicate, including a couple of music mixes on a theme he called *Old Age Ain't so Bad*.

Listening to the tapes has been an emotional experience for me. Hearing his gentle and articulate voice again lends a presence to our friendship. Discovering the tapes five years after his death is like finding a secret gift, left by a friend too unassuming to demand instant recognition and gratitude.

At another time, I will render the life story on paper so that others who lived in the neighborhood of his childhood can be provoked to remember as well. Even though I do not use his correct name herein, I still grapple with an ethical dilemma. If I publish the life story in another place, the link to this chapter, through my name, reveals that my friend was a client while I worked at the mental health center. If I completely fictionalize the names of the people and the places in the published life story, it may have some universal meaning but lose its connection to people and places that I feel need to be remembered. I suspect that the solution to this dilemma is to publish a readable transcript under my friend's name, with the family's approval, completely divorced of any connection to my name. I could never claim the publication on any resume nor could a reader trace a question or comment to me.

But does that render my friend's life meaningful to a reading audience? Likely no. As Myerhoff noted in an essay with Deena Metzger on this question, "Anthropologists talk about their natives. No one brings them in person to do rain dances at national meetings. Raw materials have no place here" (Myerhoff and Metzger 1992, 343). So we continue to struggle with the crisis of representation, no doubt. My friend is dead. He cannot provide his informed consent. My interpretation of his life cannot be confirmed nor co-authored. There is textual evidence, however, that he presumed an audience. Frequently, throughout the tapes, he makes comments such as: "listen to this," or "on this tape, we'll talk about. . . ." Moreover, he explicitly deletes major areas of his life story that he does not want to talk about because they are too painful. While I am personally familiar with those events I cannot make reference to them, out of respect for his wishes.

There are, in other words, things that are to be forgotten, but, as I reflect on the meaning of the story, the things forgotten lend meaning to the things remembered. The vividness and animation of his childhood memories stand in stark contrast to the brief and reportorial character of his summary of later life. Whole decades of his adult life are essentially elided. Yet, in his last tape, he brings his life full circle and, while sparing the details, makes reference to the role that failure has played in his life. He authors his own obituary and waxes philosophical as he reflects on his life as he has lived it, standing outside of the remembering itself.

In constructing a retrospective of his life, my friend relied on several tools. The primary tool was his own introspection, and I use the term consciously as a "looking in." Frequently, he employs visual imagination, "his mind's eye," to revisit and describe the landscape of his childhood, experienced on foot. He employs self-drawn maps to recreate the expanding automobile-supported geography of his adolescent and adult years. He uses old photos to recollect his schools, teachers, and fellow students. Old-time songs taped from the radio support his sense of what things "were like" during the Depression. Occasionally, he makes reference to conversations with his brother and phone calls with school mates that helped to confirm memories.

For the most part, he did not, however, use the physical return to origins—the proverbial Trip to Bountiful—as a technique to jog his memory. The closer he came to the end of his life, the more painful did his visits back home become, as the landscape changed, and the buildings disappeared. Increasingly, his comfort was derived from dwelling among things absent, not things present. It might be said that his childhood identity was no longer supported by the physical environment. Yet, alternatively, insofar as emotional pain was part of his adult identity, it *was* supported by the physical environment—an environment of zero signs, where the meaning (as a world lost) is derived from absences and not presences.

For many older people, the experience of moving through a changed world is precisely to experience absence and not presence. Another elder informant wrote:

> A couple of years ago, after a long absence, we made a sentimental journey to the old neighborhood and realized the truth of the saying "You can never go back." Gone was the casual and tolerant informality in lifestyles, along with the former graciousness displayed in area neighborhoods. Victorian houses had been razed and replaced by imposing new mansions, creating an atmosphere of wealth and even arrogance. New stores had ushered out the old familiar ones. New York merchants, with high-priced offerings, had moved into a huge, elaborate shopping mall a few miles distant. The lovely little village we cherished had vanished—like Brigadoon—and been replaced by ostentatious wealth and class distinction attesting to moneyed success. (Francis Sanden, in Peterson-Veatch 1995)

I do not think it is paradoxical to suggest that my friend's identity as a child and his identity as an adult were maintained concomitantly. In the privacy of his room, he was a time traveler, moving back and forth from the comfort zone of his past as reconstructed through remembering to the painful zone of his present, characterized, ironically, by absences—things he might have done. Some have argued that the work of autobiography in old age seeks continuity of self (Kaufman 1986). My friend, like Krapp, experienced discontinuity, moving to his childhood through the embodied tool of visualization, but continuingly reencountering his adult self upon reentrance into and reflection upon the present. I think he felt trapped by this paradox.

> And finally, this could well be my obituary, if they would use it, heh, I don't know if they would or not ... born July the 21st, 1920, in a house long ago torn down, to Robert and Emma Deckard, in Monroe County, was at the foot of what is known as the Chapel Hill. Of five children of Robert and Emma, two lived beyond the first few months, Jimmy W., born on the 16th of May, 1917, and myself. I spent my childhood days on Shields Ridge, from 1924, when they moved into the house there. I attended the first through 8th grade at the Poplar School and four years at Bloomington High School, graduating April the 21st, 19 and 39. [Details fictionalized]
>   The only accomplishment worth mentioning in my life is that I surpassed the allotted time that the Bible allows man, three score years and ten. And time will not permit to tell of all the blunders and mistakes in those years but I can always look back and think of what might have been.

In Wendell Berry's short novel *Remembering*, Andy Catlett, a figure quite reminiscent of my friend, struggles with the pain of self-hatred, focused on the literal loss of a member—his hand—to a corn picking machine and the figurative loss of his attachment to his own past. When experienced as something that is absent, his past brings pain, as he thinks about the good old farmer and mentor Elton Penn:

> To Andy, Elton's absence became a commanding presence. He was haunted by things he might have said to Elton that would not be sayable again in this world. That absence is with him now, but only as a weary fact, known but no longer felt, as if by some displacement of mind or heart he is growing absent from it.
>   It is the absence of everything he knows, and is known by, that surrounds him now. He is absent himself, perfectly absent. Only he knows where he is, and he is no place that he knows. His flesh feels its removal from other flesh that would recognize it or respond to its touch; it is numb with exile. He is present in his body, but his body is absent. (2002)

For Andy, recovery and redemption require remembering—remembering the long chain of personal relationships over time and centered around a place, Port William, Kentucky. It is the shades of his ancestors, not absent but present, and the world of the dead that leads him to the world of the living. The paradox is resolved as absence and presence are revealed as a unity. While my friend's obituary might suggest that he could not find the redemption that Andy Catlett found, perhaps, at times, he did. On his last tape he spoke something that he had composed and written down on the previous New Year's Day, 1991. He wrote:

> Let me do what I can, be it ever so small each day, and if the dark days of despair and depression overtake me, let me not fail to recall the strength that comforted me in the desolation of other dark days. Let me remember the bright days and hours that found me in the days gone by as I wandered in the woods behind my home on Shields Ridge and as I fished in Otter Creek with my Dad. Let me recall the comfort that would quiet my puzzled mind as I sat beside a little stream and listened to the crows in the trees overhead. . . .
>
> . . . Lift my downcast eyes upward as I jog my memory of the worth of friends, loved ones and the sunshine and the moonbeams that flow in my bedroom window as I sit here and write here today.
>
> . . . Though my sicknesses and my inabilities of these past few years tend to overtake me and I realize I have fallen so very short of the goals that I once had for myself and for my family, in days gone by, then Lord, teach me to be thankful for life and for time's golden memories that are so good and sweet and will continue to the grave.

Remembering and forgetting constitute a dialectic of presences and absences, each of which cannot exist without the other. What is said always leaves something else unsaid. Voice cannot exist without silence. As Umberto Eco notes, all signs are used to lie. As for my friend's personal memory and autobiography, it is not my place to describe things he wants forgotten to an audience he did not create. Indeed, I suspect that, for most of us, our obituaries will recount things we did and not things "we didn't." Yet, as anthropologists, who engage in cultural critique, an important role is to reveal and even resist the forces at work in the forgetting. Elie Weisel's life is a testament to the necessity of remembering. And as Cheryl Natzmer points to Pinochet's desperate plea to forget the past in order to move on (2000, 162), we realize the importance attached to our professional role and the danger of allowing the forces of forgetting to carry the day.

THE BROADER MESSAGE: PLACE MATTERS

If I have learned anything from the privileged opportunity to work with old people most of my life, it is that place matters. I suspect that I could have followed other opportunities to greener pastures (where green equals money). I recall once hearing two young business students emerging from a campus job fair, discussing their opportunities, one remarking to the other with excitement a potential job at Sara Lee. Without meaning to dampen what should be the unbridled enthusiasm of youth, I sometimes wonder if the choices we ponder over the life course might be based in more meaningful criteria than upward mobility. Perhaps we need to face down, not up. To face the ground of our existence, literally, and be more conscious about where we will dwell, what we owe to that place and not what it owes to us. As physical decline bends us forward, we have the opportunity, as in childhood, to see things close up, while, at the same time, framing our experience across a wide horizon of the future, or the past.

Aging, with its metaphor of the journey and its return, is perhaps a model for all points of life. In Chapter 1, "Being and Dwelling in Old Age," I suggested that "home is the path." Whether observing the wandering of elders with dementia or the peripatetic lives of aboriginal Australians, we create home, we make home, through going out and coming back. It is movement not stasis that creates a sense of home and belonging, whether this be physical or imaginary. It is through movement to other places and a return to our center through which we come to value the qualities of the place in which we dwell. Valuing the place is a necessary step toward the investment we make in its well-being. So we do not deserve good places so much as good places deserve us. There is a kind of reciprocal relationship we have with place that brings out the best in all of us.

We can try to design good places to grow old. We can follow the checklists. We can develop public policies that promote access, provide support, bring people into touch with each other, enable basic needs to be met. This is important work that must be done, especially in the face of the demographic imperative. However, there is another, more fundamental message here. It is not merely *what* we do but *how* we do it that matters. New Urbanists have it right to take on the physical qualities of a good neighborhood, but it takes "neighborliness" to manifest the qualities of the place. There are other intangibles discussed in this book—memory and sociability being most prominent. Good design is a necessary but not sufficient element. It is the occupation, the dwelling in a place that brings it to life—that gives it memory. Architect Emi Kiyota has described how she tries to incorporate the Japanese aesthetic of "imperfectness" in her housing design, in order to enable the occupants to fill in the meaning of a space (personal communication 2009). In wabi-sabi, the aesthetic of bonsai, true beauty blends the imperfect with the patina of age—which could certainly serve as a final design principle among those outlined in the previous chapter. If we dwell correctly, that place gives life to us and we do not exhaust its potential. And, by potential, I do not mean its "highest and best use." I refer to the root meaning of the term, L–*potens*, potency, and the force of life to sustain itself over time.

The notion of "aging in place," long a pillar of aging public policy, has been coming under some criticism of late. Some would argue that public policy should not blindly support every elder to stay in his/her home as long as physically possible (Golant 2008). I do not disagree. Indeed, I have argued that moving out at certain times in our lives is essential to the creation of perspective. Like the artist, we must wrap our eyes around something to see it in its wholeness. However, we must better appreciate how place, in its fullest sense, enters into our lives over time, as Scott Russell Sanders suggests in his foreword. It is one thing to suggest people leave a house because it has become a burden. Such a move may be advisable. It is another to expect this can happen with alacrity, especially when the alternative is merely a sterile, programmed space and not a real place that is truly open to its occupation, to its dwelling. My hope is that we do not dispense with the phrase "aging in place," as long as we understand place in its profound sense—place as an accomplishment, as movement, as investment and return.

Bibliography

AARP. 2005. *Beyond 50:05: A Report to the Nation on Livable Communities.* Washington, DC: AARP.

Abbott, Pauline S., N. Carman, J. Carman, and B. Scarfo. 2009. *Re-creating Neighborhoods for Successful Aging.* Baltimore, MD: Health Professions Press.

Alexander, Christopher, Sara Ishikawa, and Murray Silverstein. 1977. *A Pattern Language: Towns, Buildings, Construction.* New York: Oxford University Press.

Aykan, Hakan. 2003. Effect of Childlessness on Nursing Home and Home Health Care Use. *Journal of Aging and Social Policy* 15(1): 33–53.

Bachelard, Gaston (trans.). 1994. *The Poetics of Space.* Boston: Beacon.

Bahloul, Joelle. 1996. *The Architecture of Memory: A Jewish-Muslim Household in Colonial Algeria, 1937–62* (English edition). Cambridge, U.K.: Cambridge University Press.

Ball, M. Scott. 2009. Personal communication. Atlanta, GA.

Bascom, William. 1955. Verbal Art. *Journal of American Folklore* 68: 245–52.

Berry, Wendell. 1974. *The Memory of Old Jack.* San Diego: Harcourt Brace.

———. 1990. *What are People For?* San Francisco: North Point.

———. 1995. *Another Turn of the Crank.* New York: Counterpoint

———. 2002. Remembering. In *Three Short Novels.* New York: Counterpoint.

Birch, E. L. 2005. Who Lives Downtown? *Living Cities Census Series* (November). Washington, DC: The Brookings Institution.

Butrica, Barbara A., Howard M. Iams, and Karen E. Smith. 2003. It's All Relative: Understanding the Retirement Prospects of Baby-Boomers. *Center for Retirement Research Working Papers.* Boston: Boston College.

Cicourel, Aaron. 1973. *Cognitive Sociology.* London: Penguin.

Counts, Dorothy Ayers, and David R. Counts. 2001. *Over the Next Hill: An Ethnography of Senior RV'ers in North America,* 2nd edition. Peterborough: Broadview Press.

Cowgill, Donald. 1974. Aging and Modernization: A Revision of the Theory. *In Late Late: Communities and Environmental Policy*, ed. J. F. Gubrium. Springfield: Charles C. Thomas.

Csikszentmihalyi, Mihaly, and Eugene Rochberg-Halton. 1981. *The Meaning of Things: Domestic Symbols and the Self*. Cambridge: Cambridge University Press.

Cuba, L. J., and D. M. Hummon. 1993a. Constructing a Sense of Home: Place Affiliation and Migration Across the Life-Cycle. *Sociological Forum* 84: 547–72.

———. 1993b. A Place to Call Home: Identification with Dwelling Community and Religion. *The Sociological Quarterly* 34: 111–31.

d'Azevedo, Warren L. 1958. A Structural Approach to Aesthetics: Toward a Definition of Art in Anthropology. *American Anthropologist* LX: 702–14.

Doi, Takeo. 1971. *The Anatomy of Dependence*, trans. J. Bester. New York: Kodansha.

Dunham-Jones, Ellen, and June Williamson. 2009. *Retrofitting Suburbia*. Hoboken, NJ: John Wiley.

Durrett, C. 2006. *Senior Co-Housing: A Community Approach to Independent Living*. Berkeley: Ten Speed Press.

Edgerton, Robert. 1967. *The Cloak of Competence. Stigma in the Lives of the Mentally Retarded*. Berkeley: University of California.

Ekerdt, David K., and Julie F. Sargent. 2006. Family Things: Attending the Household Disbandment of Older Adults. *Journal of Aging Studies* 20: 193–205.

Feldman, Penny H., and Mia Oberlink. 2003. The AdvantAge Initiative: Developing Community Indicators to Promote the Health and Well-Being of Older People. *Family & Community Health. Community-Based Innovations in Older Populations* 26(4): 268–74.

Feldman, Penny H., Mia Oberlink, Danylle Rudin, Jane Clay, Bridget Edwards, and Philip B. Stafford. 2003. *Best Practices: Lessons for Communities in Supporting the Health, Well Being and Independence of Older People*. New York: Center for Home Care Policy and Research, Visiting Nurse Service of New York.

Feldman, Roberta M., and Lynne M. Westphal. 2000. An Agenda for Community Design and Planning: Participation and Empowerment in Practice. In *Sustaining Human Settlement: A Challenge for the New Millenium*, ed. Roderick J. Lawrence. Great Britain: Urban International Press.

Flavelle, Alix. 2002. *Community Mapping Handbook: A Guide to Making Your Own Maps of Communities and Traditional Lands*. Edmonton, AB, Canada: Lone Pine Foundation.

Foner, Nancy. 1994. *The Caregiving Dilemma: Work in an American Nursing Home*. Berkeley: University of California.

Foucault, Michel. 1979. *Discipline and Punish: The Birth of the Prison*. New York: Aldine.

Freedman, Marc. 1999. *Prime Time: How Baby Boomers Will Revolutionize Retirement and Transform America*. New York: Public Affairs.

Frey, William H. 2003. Boomers and Seniors in the Suburbs. *The Living Cities Census Series*. Washington, DC: The Brookings Institution.

———. 2006. *America's Regional Demographics in the '00s Decade: The Role of Seniors, Boomers and New Minorities*. Washington, DC: The Brookings Institution.

———. 2007. Mapping the Growth of Older America: Seniors and Boomers in the Early 21st Century. *The Living Cities Census Series*. Washington, DC: The Brookings Institution.

Garfinkel, Harold. 1967. *Studies in Ethnomethodology*. Englewood Cliffs, NJ: Prentice-Hall.

Geertz, Clifford. 1973. *The Interpretation of Cultures*. New York: Basic Books.

Gist, John R. 2007. *Population Aging, Entitlement Growth, and the Economy*. AARP Public Policy Institute #2007-01. Washington, DC: AARP.

Glassie, Henry. 1995. Home-Making: A Cross Cultural Perspective on the Conversion of Space into Place. Public Lecture. Bloomington, Indiana, April 20, 1995. Waldron Arts Center.

Goffman, Erving. 1961. *Asylums: Essays on the Social Situation of Mental Patients and Other Inmates*. Garden City, NJ: Doubleday.

———. 1963. *Behavior in Public Places*. Glencoe: Free Press.

Golant, Stephen. 2008. Low Income Elderly Homeowners in Very Old Dwellings: The Need for Public Policy Debate. *Journal of Aging and Social Policy* 20(1): 1–28.

Gubrium, Jaber. 1993. *Speaking of Life: Horizons of Meaning for Nursing Home Residents*. New York: Aldine de Gruyter.

Haas, William H., III, and William J. Serow. 2002. The Baby Boom, Amenity Retirement Migration, and Retirement Communities: Will the Golden Age of Retirement Continue? *Research on Aging* 24: 150–163.

Hanson, David, and Charles A. Emlet. 2006. Assessing a Community's Elder-Friendliness: A Case Example of the AdvantAge Initiative. *Family and Community Health* 29(4): 266–78.

Heidegger, M. 1971 (orig. 1927). Building, Dwelling, Thinking. In *Poetry, Language, Thought*, trans. A. Hofstadter. New York: Harper and Row.

Henderson, J. Neil. 1995. The Culture of Care in a Nursing Home: The Effects of a Medicalized Model of Long Term Care. In *The Culture of Long Term Care*, ed. J. Neil Henderson and Maria D. Versperi. New York: Haworth.

Henry, Jules. 1963. *Culture Against Man*. New York: Random House.

Hing, Esther. 1989. *Nursing Home Utilization by Current Residents: United States, 1985*. Hyattsville, MD: National Center for Health Statistics.

Hymes, Dell, and J. H. Gumperz. 1972. *Directions in Sociolinguistics: Ethnography of Communication*. New York: Holt, Rinehart and Winston.

Jackson, Michael. 1995. *At Home in the World*. Durham, NC: Duke University Press.

Jakobson, Roman. 1960. Closing Statement: Linquistics and Poetics. In *Style in Language*, ed. Thomas A. Sebeok. Cambridge, MA: MIT Press.

Karoly, Lynn A., and Julie Zissimopoulos. 2004. *Self-Employment and the 50+ Population*. AARP Public Policy Institute #2004-03. Washington, DC: AARP.

Katz, Stephen. 2005. *Cultural Aging: Life Course, Lifestyle, and Senior Worlds*. Orchard Park, NY: Broadview.

Kaufman, Sharon R. 1986. *The Ageless Self*. Madison, WI: University of Wisconsin Press.

Keith, Jennie. 2009. When Old Is New: Cultural Spaces and Symbolic Meaning in Late Life. In *The Cultural Context of Aging*, 3rd edition, ed. Jay Sokolovsky. Westport, CT: Praeger.

Korosec-Serfaty, Perla. 1985. Experience and Use of the Dwelling. In *Home Environments*, ed. Irwin Altman and Carol M. Werner. New York: Plenum Press.

Labov, William, and J. Waletsky. 1967. Narrative Analysis: Oral Versions of Personal Experience. In *Essays in the Verbal and Visual Arts*, ed. J. Helm. Seattle: University of Washington Press.

Lanspery, Susan, and Joan Hyde, eds. 1997. *Staying Put: Adapting the Places Instead of the People*. Amityville, NY: Baywood.

Lennertz, Bill, and A. Lutzenhiser. 2006. *The Charrette Handbook*. Chicago: American Planning Association.

Longino, Charles F., Jr., Adam T. Persynski, and Eleanor P. Stoller. 2002. Pandora's Briefcase: Unpacking the Retirement Migration Decision. *Research on Aging* 24:29–48.

Lusardi, Annamaria, and Olivia S. Mitchell. 2007. Baby Boomer Retirement Security: The Roles of Planning, Financial Literacy, and Housing Wealth. *Pension Research Council Working Paper 2007-02*. University of Pennsylvania. The Wharton School. Pension Research Council.

Maps with Teeth. 1997. Directed by Peg Campbell. Oley, PA: Bullfrog Films.

Marcoux, J. S. 2001. The "Casser Maison" Ritual: Constructing the Self by Emptying the Home. *Journal of Material Culture* 6:213–35.

Marcus, Claire Cooper. 1995. *House as a Mirror of Self: Exploring the Deeper Meaning of Home*. Berkeley, CA: Conari Press.

McCamant, K., and C. Durrett. 1994. *Co-Housing: A Contemporary Approach to Housing Ourselves*. Berkeley: Habitat Press.

McHugh, Kevin E., and Robert C. Mings. 1996. The Circle of Migration: Attachment to Place in Aging. *Annals of the Association of American Geographers* 86(3): 530–50.

Meltzer, Graham. 2005. *Sustainable Community: Learning from the Cohousing Model*. Victoria, CA: Trafford.

Mermin, Gordon B. T., Richard W. Johnson, and Dan P. Murphy. 2007. Why do Boomers Plan to Work Longer? *Journal of Gerontology* 62B(5): S286–S294.

Moody, Harry R. 1986. The Meaning of Life and the Meaning of Old Age. In *What Does It Mean to Grow Old: Reflections from the Humanities*, ed. Thomas R. Cole and Sally Gadow. Durham, NC: Duke University Press.

Moore, James F., and Olivia S. Mitchell. 1997. Projected Retirement Wealth and Savings Adequacy in the Health and Retirement Study. *Working Paper* 6240. Cambridge, MA: National Bureau of Economic Research.

Morgan, David L., and Richard A. Krueger. 1998. *The Focus Group Kit.* Thousand Oaks, CA: Sage Publications.

Myerhoff, Barbara. 1978. *Number Our Days.* New York: Simon and Schuster.

Myerhoff, Barbara, and Deena Metzger. 1992. The Journal as Activity and as Genre. In *Remembered Lives: The Work of Ritual, Storytelling, and Growing Older*, ed. Barbara Myerhoff. Ann Arbor: University of Michigan.

National Association of Area Agencies on Aging. 2007. *A Blueprint for Action: Developing a Livable Community for All Ages.* Washington, DC.

Natzmer, Cheryl. 2002. Remembering and Forgetting: Creative Expression and Reconciliation in Post-Pinochet Chile. In *Social Memory and History: Anthropological Perspectives*, ed. J. Climo and M. G. Cattell. Walnut Creek, CA: Altimira.

Oberlink, Mia, and Philip B. Stafford. Forthcoming. Community Planning with and for Older Adults. *Generations: Journal of the American Society on Aging.*

Oldenburg, Ray. 1999. *The Great Good Place*, 3rd edition. New York: Marlowe.

Peterson, Jane W. 1997. Age of Wisdom: Elderly Black Women in Family and Church. In *The Cultural Context of Aging: Worldwide Perspectives*, ed. J. Sokolovsky. Westport, CT: Bergin and Garvey.

Peterson, Peter. 1999. *The Gray Dawn: How the Coming Age Wave Will Transform America—and the World.* New York: Random House.

Peterson-Veatch, E., ed. 1995. *Experiencing Place.* Bloomington, IN: Bloomington Hospital.

Race, Bruce, and Carolyn Torma. 1998. *Youth Planning Charrettes.* Chicago: American Planning Association.

Regnier, Victor, and Jon Pynoos. 1987. *Housing the Aged: Design Directives and Policy Considerations.* New York: Elsevier.

Rosenbaum, Mark S. 2006. Exploring the Social Supportive Role of Third Places in Consumers' Lives. *Journal of Service Research* 9: 59–72.

Sacks, Harvey. 1974. A Simplest Systematics for the organization of Turn-Taking in Conversation. *Language* 50(4): 696–735.

Sanders, Scott Russell. 1993. *Staying Put: Making a Home in a Restless World.* Boston: Beacon.

Schuchat. Molly. 1995. Personal Communication.

Sharoff, Robert. Retirees Find Housing at Their Alma Maters. *The New York Times*, September 23, 2007. http://www.nytimes.com/2007/09/23/realestate/23nati.html?_r=1.

Shield, Renee Rose. 1988. *Uneasy Endings: Daily Life in an American Nursing Home*. Ithaca, NY: Cornell.

Shumway, J. Matthew, and Samuel M. Otterstrom. 2001. Spatial Patterns of Migration and Income Change in the Mountain West: The Dominance of Service-Based, Amenity Rich Counties. *Professional Geographer* 53(4): 492–502.

Silverman, Myrna, and Carol McCallister. 1995. Continuities and Discontinuities in the Life Course: Experiences of Demented Persons in a Residential Alzheimer's Facility. In *The Culture of Long Term Care*, ed. J. Neil Henderson and Maria Vesperi. Westport, CT: Bergin and Garvey.

Silverman, Philip, ed. 1987. *The Elderly as Modern Pioneers*. Bloomington: Indiana University.

Silverman, P., and R. Maxwell. 1983. The Significance of Information and Power in the Comparative Study of the Aged. In *Growing Old in Different Societies: Cross Cultural Perspectives*, ed. Jay Sokolovsky. Acton, MA: Copley.

Simmel, George. 1971 (orig. 1915). *On Individuality and Social Forms: Selected Writings*, ed. Donald Levine. Chicago: University of Chicago Press.

Slim, H., and P. Thompson. 1995. *Listening for a Change: Oral Testimony and Community Development*. London: New Society.

Snyder, Gary. 1990. *The Practice of the Wild*. San Francisco: North Point Press.

Stafford, Philip. 1996. *The Evergreen Household Survey*. Bloomington: Evergreen Institute.

———. 2001. When Community Planning Becomes Community Building: Place-Based Activism and the Creation of Good Places to Grow Old. In *Empowering Frail Elderly People*, ed. L. F. Heumann, M. E. McCall, and D. P. Boldy. Wesport, CT: Praeger.

———. 2003. Homebodies: Voices of Place in a North American Community. In *Gray Areas: Ethnographic Encounters with Nursing Home Culture*, ed. Philip B. Stafford. Santa Fe, NM: SAR Press.

———. 2006. Creating Lifespan Communities. In *Public Policy and Aging Report* 15: 4. Gerontological Society of America: National Academy on an Aging Society.

———. 2009. Aging in the Hood: Creating and Sustaining Elder Friendly Environments. In *The Cultural Context of Aging: Worldwide Perspectives*. Jay Sokolovsky, ed. Westport, CT: Praeger.

———. 2009. Living Large while Living Small: The Spatial Life of Aging Boomers. In *Boomer Bust? Economic and Political Issues of the Graying Society*, ed. Robert B. Hudson. Westport, CT: Praeger.

Stafford, Philip B., Inta Carpenter, and David Taylor. 2004. Documenting Local Culture: An Introductory Field School. In *Passages: The Ethnographic Field*

School and First Fieldwork Experiences, ed. M. Iris. Chicago: National Association for the Practice of Anthropology Bulletin No. 22.

Surowiecki, James. 2004. *The Wisdom of Crowds*. New York: Random House.

Thomas, William H. 2004. *What Are Old People For? How Elders Will Save the World*. Acton, MA: VanderWyk and Burnham.

Tuan, Yi-Fu. 1977. *Space and Place: The Perspective of Experience*. Minneapolis: University of Minnesota Press.

Turner, Victor. 1977. *The Ritual Process*. Ithaca, NY: Cornell University Press.

U.S. Census. 2008. *Facts for Features: U.S. Age Projections*. CB08-FF0.6. Washington, DC.

Verbrugge, L., and A. Jette. 1994. The Disablement Process. *Social Science and Medicine* 38(1): 1–14.

Walters, William H. 2002. Place Characteristics and Later-Life Migration. *Research on Aging* 24: 243–76.

Whyte, William H. 1988. *City: Rediscovering the Center*. New York: Anchor Books.

Woodward, Kathleen. 1986. Reminiscence and the Life Review: Prospects and Retrospects. In *What Does It Mean to Grow Old? Reflections from the Humanities*, ed. Thomas R. Cole and Sally Gadow. Durham, NC: Duke University Press.

———. 1991. *Aging and Its Discontents: Freud and Other Fictions*. Bloomington: Indiana University Press.

Wright, Scott D., Michael Caserta, and Dale A. Lund. 2003. Older Adults' Attitudes, Concerns and Support for Environmental Issues in the "New West." *International Journal of Aging and Human Development* 57(2): 151–79.

Index

About the Author

PHILIP B. STAFFORD, Ph.D., directs the Center on Aging and Community at the Indiana Institute on Disability and Community (Indiana University). A cultural anthropologist, he received his B.A. from the University of Chicago, and his Ph.D. from Indiana University. In Indiana, Stafford has been instrumental in developing a wide range of programs for older persons and has organized numerous statewide training events. At the national and international level, he is active in research, speaking, and publishing around issues of community development for elder-friendly communities. He is a senior consultant with the AdvantAge Initiative, a national project that has supported community planning for aging in nearly 30 U.S. communities. He is a founding board member with Memory Bridge, the Foundation for Alzheimer's and Cultural Memory, and the author of numerous articles and book chapters. He is the editor of *Gray Areas: Ethnographic Encounters with Nursing Home Culture* (SAR Press, 2003).